Systems Programmer's
PROBLEM SOLVER

WINTHROP COMPUTER SYSTEMS SERIES

Gerald M. Weinberg, *editor*

MOSTELLER
Systems Programmer's Problem Solver

HEALEY AND HEBDITCH
The Minicomputer in On-Line Systems

CONWAY, GRIES, AND ZIMMERMAN
A Primer on PASCAL, 2nd ed.

BASSO AND SCHWARTZ
Programming with FORTRAN/WATFOR/WATFIV

SHNEIDERMAN
Software Psychology: Human Factors in Computer and Information Systems

GRAYBEAL AND POOCH
Simulation: Principles and Methods

WALKER
Problems for Computer Solutions Using FORTRAN

WALKER
Problems for Computer Solutions Using BASIC

CHATTERGY AND POOCH
Top-down, Modular Programming in FORTRAN with WATFIV

LINES AND BOEING
Minicomputer Systems

GREENFIELD
Architecture of Microcomputers

NAHIGIAN AND HODGES
Computer Games for Businesses, Schools, and Homes

MONRO
Basic BASIC

CONWAY AND GRIES
An Introduction to Programming:
A Structured Approach Using PL/I and PL/C, 3rd ed.

CONSTABLE AND O'DONNELL
A Programming Logic

CRIPPS
An Introduction to Computer Hardware

COATS AND PARKIN
Computer Models in the Social Sciences

EASLEY
Primer for Small Systems Management

CONWAY
A Primer on Disciplined Programming Using PL/I, PL/CS, and PL/CT

FINKENAUR
COBOL for Students: A Programming Primer

WEINBERG, WRIGHT, KAUFFMAN, AND GOETZ
High Level Cobol Programming

CONWAY AND GRIES
Primer on Structured Programming Using PL/I, PL/C, and PL/CT

GILB AND WEINBERG
Humanized Input: Techniques for Reliable Keyed Input

William S. Mosteller
Boeing Computer Services Company

Systems Programmer's
PROBLEM SOLVER

Winthrop Publishers, Inc.
Cambridge, Massachusetts

Library of Congress Cataloging in Publication Data

Mosteller, William
    Systems programmer's problem solver.

    Includes index.
    1. Electronic digital computers — Programming.
I. Title.
QA76.6.M68   001.64′2   81-821
ISBN 0-87626-830-0   AACR2

Illustrations by: **H. R. Russell**

© 1981 by Winthrop Publishers, Inc.
   17 Dunster Street, Cambridge, Massachusetts   02138

10 9 8 7 6 5 4 3 2 1

To Pat

Contents

Foreword   xi
Preface   xiii

    Introduction   1

1. Debugging   3

Trampled Data   5
Traps   7
Save the Dump   9
What Did You Change Recently?   10
What Is the Program Doing?   11
Special Debugging Tools   13
Instrumentation   16
Corrective Redesign   17
Nothing Changed   19
Absolute Patches   20
Hardware Monitor   22
"Waste" a Little Machine Time   26
Vendor Support   27
Automating the Arithmetic   29
Enqueue Lockouts   30
Reading Code   33
Did You Use the Same Model Throughout?   34
Timing Problems   35

It Must Be Hardware!   36
Save Area Mismanagement   41
Loops   43
Follow-up   46

2. Operating Procedures and Tools   47

Clean Dumps   49
Console Message Logs   50
Maintenance and Failure Logs   51
No One Else Has Reported This Problem   52
Extract Routines   53
Peripheral Power   54
Better Terminals   56
Home Terminals   58
Manuals   61
Follow-up   65

3. Prevention   67

Structured Walkthroughs   69
Plan for Debugging   71
Avoiding Yesterday's Efficiency   73
Fast Assembler Language Coding   75
Tight Use of Memory   77
Use Higher Level Languages   79
Portability   81
"Efficient" Coding in Higher Level Languages   83
Processor Recovery   85
Don't Skimp on Operator Commands   87
User Documentation   88
What's Wrong With Flowcharts   90
Decision Tables   92
Error Messages   95
Abend   98
Response Messages   99
Humane Input   101
Automatic Spelling Correction   104
Top Down Implementation   106

What About Dataset Security?   108
Sunset Support   109
Modular Changes   111
Simulation   113
Follow-up   115

4. Coding Practices   117

Structured Programming   119
Quirks of Assembler Language   120
Smelling Dead Fish   125
Use Memory Protect   126
SVC 255   127
Reentrency   129
Dynamic Instruction Modification   131
Special Instruction Sets   133
Memory Management   134
Comments in Assembler Language   136
Eliminate the Diagnostics   139
What Version of the Program Is This?   141
Follow-up   143

5. Keeping It Symbolic   145

The Current Location Counter, *   147
Mapping Macros   149
Device Dependency   151
Don't Count Characters   154
Assembly Parameters   156
Follow-up   157

6. Testing   159

Planning the Test   161
The Quick Test   163
Test the Original Function   165
Retesting   166

Fast Clocks and Counters   167
Restrictive Environments   168
Test Every Branch   169
Stress Testing   171
Data File Acceptance Testing   172
Methodic Testing   175
System Testing   176
Follow-up   178

7. Management   179

System Documentation   181
User Group Meetings   182
Conference Trip Report   184
System Integrity   186
Fear of Falling   188
Making It Beautiful   190
Project Planning   191
Shifts in Specifications   192
Building Versus Buying Software   195
Teamwork   198
Using a New Systems Programmer   200
The Annual Report   202
Firefighting Without Burning Out   204
Demonstrations   208
Follow-up   210

Afterword   211

Appendix A   Enqueue Lockout Prevention   213

Appendix B   Assembler Language Danger Areas   215

Appendix C   Economics of Systems Programmers   217

Glossary   219

Index   221

Foreword

When I lived in Switzerland as a child and played soccer, the boys were always amused by my clumsy feet, and amazed by my adroit hands. European children are conditioned *never* to put their hands on the ball, unless they are destined to become goalkeepers. In the same way, today's programmers are conditioned *never* to put their hands on the machine — unless they are destined to become systems programmers.

You can always tell which boys will grow up to be goalies. They stand a bit apart from the others, they don't laugh at the same bungled plays, and they have a perpetually worried look in their eyes. When working in the goalmouth, with the ball at the other end of the field, they're always sweeping away imaginary bits of paper and manicuring stray tufts of grass that might deflect an enemy shot by a quarter of a millimeter. I think that systems programmers, too, may be a breed apart, with many of the same characteristics. Like the goalie, the systems programmer is the last line of defense against a tragedy too horrible for others to contemplate. Like the goalies, they appear to be doing little, but are always preparing for rare events while their teammates run up and down the field, kicking, shouting, and expending energy.

I don't know how goalkeepers learn to be goalkeepers. I know they don't learn from books. It's almost as hard to find a book on goal tending as it is to find one on systems programming. Oh yes, there are books with the words "systems programming" in the title, but they all turn out to be about data structures, or how to write compilers and operating systems. The systems programmer who writes a compiler is as rare as the goalie who kicks goals. The role played by systems programmers is defense, not offense; they protect the millions of ordinary programmers from the most dangerous shots of nature, hardware, and the software vendors. Systems programmers — like goalies — never seem to be appreciated, or even noticed, until the defense breaks down. But when things go wrong, so they're noticed, they've already failed. Now with the publication of William Mosteller's book, systems programmers may begin to get some of the notice and appreciation they deserve from regular programmers.

Of course *Systems Programmer's Problem Solver* wasn't written for the regular programmers, but, rather for the systems programmers themselves. As it happens, they're as much in the dark about one another's work as anybody. Yet they stand to gain much more from enlightenment.

When systems programmers get together, they love to share their accumulated knowledge. But most systems programmers are too busy protecting the goal to go out and share secrets. Hence the value of this compendium of practical systems programming experience. Out of his bag of special tricks, Mosteller has abstracted a collection of generally applicable ideas that no systems programmer can afford to ignore. No doubt each practitioner knows many of these techniques, but there can't be more than a handful of systems programmers who won't find at least one idea for saving $1,000 and a night's sleep.

Then there are the *new* systems programmers, who can best be described by the word "overwhelmed." I would strongly recommend that every new systems programmer be handed a copy of *Systems Programmer's Problem Solver* along with the yellow promotion slip. A pleasant Sunday evening curled up in a comfortable chair with Mosteller's book will convert that first Monday from a nightmare into a pleasant and profitable learning experience.

And if you ever hear programmers or managers mutter, "just what do systems programmers *do*, anyway?", rush out and get them copies of *Systems Programmer's Problem Solver* for their very own. They may not understand every word, but just for a moment they may comprehend what it's like to stand alone, watched by thousands of screaming fans, protecting the goal.

GERALD M. WEINBERG

Series Editor

Preface

I intend for this book to make life easier for systems programmers. System reliability is critical to the success of our industry, and you *can* have a reliable system. The techniques described below will guide you.

For the past few years, I have worked mainly on IBM System/360 and S/370 computers, installing and modifying the JES2 (and its predecessor, HASP) spooling system and the TSO terminal system. I have solved many program failures, and most of my training in problem resolution came from helpful friends or my own discoveries.

A body of literature is beginning to appear supporting improved debugging. Several authors refer to Strunk and White, *The Elements of Style* (New York: Macmillan, 1972), and recommend the same goals of simplicity and clarity of expression in computer languages as in English. Kernighan and Plauger's *The Elements of Programming Style*, 2d. ed. (New York: McGraw-Hill, 1978), Ledgard's *Programming Proverbs* (Rochelle Park, N.J.: Hayden Book Company, 1975), and Weinberg's *The Psychology of Computer Programming* (New York: Van Nostrand Reinhold, 1971) all address weaknesses of program style affecting correct program operation. My "Coding Practices" section has the same theme, but is oriented toward assembler language programming.

However, the operating systems programmer facing a system crash needs something more. News that better coding practices would have prevented the problem doesn't help. Our programmer may not even have developed the code. Unfortunately, we cannot simply wish away our real need to debug. Van Tassel's

Program Style, Design, Efficiency, Debugging and Testing, 2d.
ed. (Englewood Cliffs, N.J.: Prentice-Hall, 1978) takes us the
entire way from design to production and Glass's *Software Reliability Guidebook* (Englewood Cliffs, N.J.: Prentice-Hall, 1979)
gives a thorough treatment of software reliability techniques and
tools, but neither is primarily oriented toward operating system
programming.

To best use this book, the student needs to know assembler language† and have some experience with operating system
modifications.

IBM System/370 assembler language is used where an
example would help illustrate a point. I considered whether to
use a real computer or an abstract machine and settled on the
/370 because of my familiarity with it, because of the large number of System/370 systems programmers, and because I know
of no universally accepted method for writing assembler language
illustrations. The several different models make the System/370
series an abstract machine.

At the end of each section, a chapter entitled "Follow-
up" contains thought questions and exercises intended to slow
your pace through the book and increase your benefits from the
reading. The index should allow you to refer back to specific
topics without having to search the book sequentially. The layout
we have chosen includes blank space throughout the book to let
you to write notes about the material. You are encouraged to
write me, care of the publisher, if you have strong feelings (negative or positive) about anything you read here.

Many people made this book possible. I am indebted to
my parents, Virginia and Frederick Mosteller, for lifelong help
and encouragement. In addition, my father worked over the draft
with vigor and thoroughness, and the improvements are striking.
Years ago he taught me that although the first draft is a milestone,
it probably won't resemble the finished product. Sarah Fleming,
Morton Hoffman, Gale Mosteller, Keith Reynolds, Patricia
Thompson, and Gerald Weinberg each reviewed the draft, suggesting many major improvements. Patricia Mosteller and Virginia Mosteller proofread the book as well. Richard Olson pro-

---

† Two texts have been recommended: George W. Struble, *Assembler
Language Programming: the IBM System/360 and 370*, 2d. ed. (Reading, Mass.:
Addison-Wesley, 1975) and Kevin McQuillen, Mike Murach, ed., *System/360-
370 Assembler Language (OS)* (Fresno, Calif.: Mike Murach & Associates, 1975).

vided considerable help with the literature survey. All this support has improved the book, but I must take the blame for any shortcomings that remain.

At the University of Pennsylvania Computer Center, between 1965 and 1968, I first worked in systems programming and met System/360. Since 1971, my experiences at Boeing Computer Services Company have been even more stimulating. These employers contributed positively to my career and knowledge.

Boeing Computer Services Company, and especially Sy Listman and Ron Geiger, provided valuable support for this project. Of special importance, the book was entered and edited, and drafts printed using BCS' MAINSTREAM®-TSO system, greatly simplifying preparation. Of course, the opinions and conclusions are mine, rather than BCS'. Reference to specific hardware or software vendors' offerings in this book does not imply BCS endorsement of their use.

Finally, my wife, Pat, and stepson, Jeff Olson, have improved my life dramatically. My first ideas for the book date back a few years, but only since our marriage have I been able to complete it. Our happy home life made it possible.

I hope these ideas make you more efficient and that you enjoy reading and using this book as much as I enjoyed writing it.

WILLIAM MOSTELLER

Falls Church, Virginia

® MAINSTREAM is a registered servicemark of the Boeing Company.

Introduction

Recent work in computer science has produced techniques for proving, mathematically, the correctness of programs. The techniques are currently too time-consuming and difficult for most applications, but are being used to develop the security kernel (central nucleus) for some secure operating systems.†

Until these techniques become more usable, most of us will have to debug programs in the same manner we always have. Fortunately, we can work faster than before. Don't prepare yourself for a pep talk: I am not going to demand that you work harder, rather I am going to present methods of working *smarter*. The methods described here have been proven under fire.

I confess that, when speaking of operating systems programming, "computer science" sounds, to me, suspiciously like a word pairing, like "jumbo shrimp," that doesn't naturally fit together! I believe that much of our work will continue to be a craft rather than a science for some time. However, an activity can undergo dramatic changes and still remain a craft. The theme of this book is that systems programmers, as craftsmen, can improve their methods as dramatically as printing changed: from monks illuminating manuscripts to printing presses using movable type. We will repeatedly see changes in technique that dramatically reduce our labor costs.

---

†For a good survey of this work, see Ruth Nelson and Joseph Jarzembowski, "Multilevel Security: An Overview and New Directions," presented at "Trends & Applications 1977: Computer Security and Integrity," May 19, 1977, Gaithersburg, MD. Symposium Proceedings available from the IEEE, 5855 Naples Plaza, Suite 301, Long Beach, CA 90803.

1

The "Debugging" section of the book describes methods to resolve your current system problems. The "Procedures and Tools" section suggests production runs and standard practices that will make debugging easier. The "Prevention" and "Coding Practices" sections detail techniques that will reduce errors in new modifications you develop, while the "Keeping it Symbolic" section will help you avoid writing overly specific assembler language code. The "Testing" section shows ways to detect program errors. The "Management" section discusses important issues that are only partly technical. Don't take these categories too seriously. I encourage you to dip in anywhere. I once used both a structured walkthrough and a decision table (under "Prevention") as debugging tools.

SECTION 1

Debugging

The goal in solving a system problem is to move from the reason for the failure, the undesirable result, to the underlying, often well hidden cause. Most failures can be traced immediately from the result to the cause. A good example is an instruction interrupt when running a newly assembled program. The assembler generates a string of zeros for an uninterpretable source instruction, and zero is an invalid operation code. Note that the effect, an instruction interrupt, differs from the cause, incorrect assembler language syntax.

Although the difference between cause and effect will be seen again and again, this example is not very challenging, because the effect leads us immediately to the cause. In tougher problems, the cause and effect may be separated widely, either by time or memory location.

I will be rash here and state that any problem that can be made to occur can be fixed. Before I get into trouble, I better say that the fix may require a complete redesign of the function involved, but when a known set of conditions produces a problem, the problem can be diagnosed. If we know that a specific, defined set of actions yields a failure, we can use straightforward techniques to diagnose the problem.

The worst trouble, then, comes with problems that we cannot readily reproduce. These, too, are predictable but occur only under circumstances that are hard to create, for example, because they need an especially high or peculiar system load. If we cannot reproduce a problem, we must intercept its seemingly random occurrences to gather information. Because we

3

cannot produce the failure under circumstances we control, diagnosis is more expensive, and resolution is delayed.

The methods discussed in this section will improve your ability to collect information about program failures, and thus ease problems associated with developing corrections.

Trampled Data

Overlays (good data trampled by bad) are a common cause of failures. Generally, the program uses a pointer incorrectly, and places something specific at a particular offset in the wrong control block. (With luck, the data inserted will have a recognizable pattern, perhaps suggesting its origin. Unfortunately, luck is often unreliable: the overlay may be a string of zeros.)

When coding a routine that references control blocks, be sure to use a base register (on a 370, base register zero means the first 4096 bytes of memory, where overlays are disastrous) and be sure to use the right one.

Wrong Control Block

When you think you are referring to a long control block, but instead are incorrectly referencing a shorter one, you may overlay the next (not the current) control block. With groups of control blocks that are contiguous in memory, the overlay will not immediately be detected. The delay makes this error a very frustrating variation.

Too Long a Data Field

Length problems can also cause trouble when you are pointing to the correct block. A buffer often has a fixed format header

with control information, including a buffer chain field. The buff-
ered text follows. If you move too much data into the buffer,
the control information at the head of the next buffer, including
the chain field, is destroyed. The overlay is often not detected
until much later, when the damaged chain field is next used.

Trampled Code

Sometimes an overlay will damage code, rather than data. When
program operation defies reasonable logic, compare the code in
storage with the program listing. Here again, the timing of the
overlay may be well separated from the resultant failure. Don't
forget to check your literals, and other assembled data, for
damage.

With data overlays, the program failure frequently occurs
well after the fact. Direct means often do not lead us from effect
to cause, and "Traps," described in the next chapter, are required to detect the cause of our problem.

Traps

As pointed out earlier, the goal in a debugging situation is to move from the failure to the cause. Sometimes we can only get closer (in time) to the cause. A failure that can be detected earlier can often be corrected. Traps allow us to move back in time.

Typically, service routines perform validity checking of their input. They *trap* illogical input and avoid taking incorrect actions. Frequently, range checking is used: if functions are selected with a branch table, test for a function number outside the supported range before blithely branching based on the supplied number. If you know the memory range where a control block must reside, check that the pointer supplied is within the appropriate range. Some thought must, of course, be given to the performance implications of such a trap. The more frequently the routine is used, the more costly validity checking becomes.

Avoid developing a trap that does not move closer to the problem. For example, a trap that turns a loop into a immediate program failure usually does not help the debugging process, because only the time needed to detect the loop has been saved. When sprung, a trap should teach us something new about a failure. One which only offers faster recovery usually moves us no closer to resolution.

By following five steps, you can prepare a trap.

1. Study the failure (result) thoroughly.
2. Follow the program logic backwards, using whatever information is available.

3. Select one or more spots where you believe earlier detection of the problem is possible.

4. Determine what sort of action the trap should take. Ideally the trap will capture enough data to allow immediate problem resolution. To ensure this, we must leave nothing to chance: automatically dumping the contents of storage we wish to examine is ideal, since then we do not rely on an operator to take the proper action. Unfortunately our concept of what storage we wish to examine can change once we examine it, requiring further dumping. Halting the system may allow us to examine storage from the console, but on larger systems this practice is discouraged, and may be no help if we are not present when the halt occurs. Simply sending a message to the log usually will not capture enough data, and may upset and confuse the operator. No one likes to see a message of the form: "Something scary happened in module X in routine Y."

5. Code and test traps appropriate for the spots you have selected.

Test your traps. Make certain the trap you have developed will detect abnormal conditions, and not simply unusual, but normal, system operation. For example, if the editor was occasionally ending without saving the updated file, a trap might be appropriate. This trap would have to check for user requested termination without file saving to prevent intercepting this normal condition. A trap that closes on non-problems is not helpful. If the trap affects a heavily used system routine, comparing system performance before and after the trap is installed will give some concrete data about impact.

These five steps will help you to write good traps in any situation. The data the traps produce will at least allow you to write more refined traps, and ultimately solve the problem.

Save the Dump

Sometimes (rarely, I hope) you will have a problem that the tricks I have described do not help you solve. Use my last chance, desperation method of solving the problem.

Used improperly, this approach can be a major avoidance technique, preventing resolution of any system problems. Used properly, however, it allows the problem solver to accumulate two or three different failures with the same external symptoms. While a unique occurrence of a problem may be impossible to solve, two or three allow you to identify similarities, develop hypotheses and therefore traps, and get closer to the failure. Let us hope the problem will not require twenty or thirty saved dumps to resolve. You may need special storage techniques: magnetic tapes or microfiche, while less convenient than paper, are less trouble than a large number of thick listings.

If the problem occurs only once a month, saving the dump may be one technique you will need to solve it. Unfortunately an extraordinarily reliable system can only come from solving the rarer, harder problems.

What Did You Change Recently?

Program changes often cause unexpected troubles, sometimes well removed from the specific change. Beyond insufficient checking of the change being installed, other pitfalls are perhaps a little less obvious. If object card decks are being used, a card may be lost. The linkage editor and loader you use may not check for missing cards or cards out of sequence.

I once changed a program and it stopped working completely. Hours of painful, frustrating, infuriating research disclosed an undocumented sensitivity to the presence or absence of *System Status Information* on the load module. My link-edit input lacked a SETSSI control card.

In modifying a large program, USING new base registers (for code or control blocks) and omitting the subsequent DROP can cause code many lines later in the module, unrelated to your change, to use the wrong base register. By convention, when two USINGs are outstanding for the same area, the assembler chooses the higher numbered register. Thus the odds are only 50:50 that a missing DROP will not affect later code.

The general rule is to ask what you have done to the program recently, since recent changes often cause failures. Research scientists keep hard-bound logs of their experimental work; the systems programmer could similarly log what is being done. Simply writing down what you are attempting may save an otherwise wasted computer run.

What Is the Program Doing?

Avoid getting bogged down in the details of a problem or you may miss the point. A good rule is to look over all the data available (instruction counter, registers, save areas, program storage, and program output) to determine where the program should be. When the data disagree, the instruction counter is suspect.

The question then is how did we get here? Here is the sequence we follow to find the failing instruction:

1. Since BAL and BALR instructions are common, we need to check the registers. Return addresses left in registers, particularly register 14, show the last subroutine call executed. We then check whether we have returned from the subroutine.

2. Once we have found the last subroutine call, we can examine the other registers in light of the code near the subroutine call and within the subroutine to determine what instructions have already been executed.

3. Finally, we can examine appropriate data areas (those used by the program segment we are looking at) to determine more closely what instructions have been executed.

This sequence should lead us to the failing instruction, probably a branch instruction using a bad address or perhaps bad data in a register. Following the save area chain can also give clues. If the machine has a stack (370's do not) it will help you follow the program path.

Beware excessive reliance on the instruction counter. With wild transfers, such reliance hinders debugging. A global view of the failure allows us to resolve it more quickly.

Special Debugging Tools

No job is easy when we lack the necessary tools. Frequently special programs will ease debugging. Three specific types of programs help us the most: dump printing programs, *debuggers,* and tracing programs.

Dump Printers

The first debugging tool that comes to mind is the dump printing program. Generally a dump is easier to solve if the control blocks are neatly formatted, rather than just printed as they appear in memory. The OS/VS dump printing program supports *exits* to do this; the time spent writing or finding and installing an exit tailored to specific needs is quickly recovered with time saved looking at dumps. The less time spent on drudgery, such as running control block chains, the faster the problem gets fixed.

Debuggers

A dynamic debugging aid† can save you a lot of time. A good one sets *breakpoints* to halt execution for examination and mod-

---

†A good one for OS/VS systems, DBC, is available through Yale University Computer Center, 175 Whitney Avenue, New Haven, CT 06520.

13

ification of program and data. Such programs have a special syntax you must learn, but once passed that, their use is natural and efficient. Some systems offer only a debugger and no dump program. The debugger may include symbol table support, so that you may use program labels during debugging.

Often a debugger may be used instead of a dump program. If the debugger supports a symbol table, the storage prints it makes will include symbolic information and thus be more readable. A debugger can take you straight to the problem, with much less output, improving your debugging speed and helping the environment. The reduced output means a narrower window through which to examine the problem and can cause you to miss information adjacent to the data areas you examine with the debugger. You may sometimes wish to print a dump of a problem instead of using a debugger to allow you to view more information.

The debugger shows its greatest strength when used to monitor program execution. The ability to run an executing program and watch internal operations gives you considerable power. The technique is similar to that used by a mountain climber crossing a sheer rock face: breakpoints are the pitons, you inch through the program, executing small sections and then examining registers and storage to assure that all is well.

Tracers

A relative of the dynamic debugger is the tracing program, which records events occurring during program operation. Although less flexible and passive in nature, traces can be useful. Used indiscriminately, however, trace programs can create wastefully large piles (pounds) of output. At today's computing speeds, tracing each instruction executed during a second of machine time means nearly a million lines of output!

All these tools can make life much easier, once they are mastered. However, one must, in some cases, get past the prejudice that sometimes, unaccountably, surrounds such packages. (True-to-life dialogue with a systems programmer:

"Why isn't TESTRAN† installed?"
"It doesn't work."
"How do you know?"
"Joe tried it 5 years ago.")

You cannot afford not to know what tools are available for your work. Take some time to learn how to use the debugging programs at your command.

---

†TESTRAN was a batch debugging system for OS/360. Its use has been supplanted by interactive debuggers such as the TSO TEST command and DBC (see preceding note).

Instrumentation

Large systems often rely on critical internal resources: buffers and control blocks whose usage cannot easily be tracked externally. Instead of laboriously reviewing storage dumps for this information, add a resource monitor to the system. The monitor does the same counting you would do manually using the dump, and reports the results, either automatically or on request. The programming effort needed to install such instrumentation is often astonishingly small, particularly compared to the benefits.

Although I had used JES2 and HASP for several years, I only slowly realized our need for instrumentation to monitor counts of the buffers and control blocks available. I sometimes discovered, well after the fact, that a particular failure was caused by a resource shortage.

Finally I designed and a co-worker wrote the routine. A new JES2 command invokes resource counting, and the results are reported to the console operator and recorded on the accounting file. Implementation by command allows us to quickly determine whether a system problem is due to a resource shortage, and we can respond more intelligently. The command is issued automatically during the day, and a post-processor prepares reports from the recorded data. The coding effort was about three person-months' work, and the benefits are enormous. The eight pages of code have paid for themselves many times over. I wonder how we survived without them.

Software instrumentation need not mean a large or complicated development effort: a simple tool is often all you need and is infinitely better than no tool at all.

16

Corrective Redesign

System code often develops tenure at an installation. Years after the code's original environment has changed or disappeared, the code, patched and fixed, continues to limp along. When a program can be maintained and modified by only one particular individual on the staff, corrective redesign is indicated. (See "Prevention" for some ideas about how to avoid recreating the problem.) It takes firm resolve to shoot these injured horses, but the benefits are considerable.

Our stable once included one. In converting from BCRE (our roll-your-own teleprocessing system) to IBM's TSO, a coworker developed a command for job output retrieval. The command attempted to mimic BCRE's interface to HASP, but failed. TSO's use of swapping, *SMF* accounting, and our poor understanding of the archaic, complicated, undocumented interface combined to produce lockouts and low storage overlays. (The interface had passed the redesign test just mentioned, and more, as nobody in the shop fully understood the code.) It became our major reliability problem overnight. Standard debugging techniques repeatedly failed to provide relief, so, in desperation, we started from scratch.

I developed a completely new interface replacing both the TSO and HASP code. The new interface was designed to make the existing failures impossible. All movement of data (with one exception) was performed under the TSO storage protect key to prevent inadvertent overlays. All WAITs were protected by watchdog timers, allowing detection of lost POST conditions.

Carefully prepared flowcharts and thorough walkthroughs eliminated many problems during design.

The replacement code was such a success we marveled that it took us so long to realize the need. (In its entire life, the new code cost us one system crash, compared with roughly two per day for the old interface.) We had tricked ourselves into thinking that a couple thousand lines of code had value far beyond their actual replacement cost, and had therefore avoided writing the much needed replacement.

Nothing Changed

Perhaps the most frustrating part of programming is writing an enormous change, installing it, and testing it, only to discover that the new code works *exactly* like the old. No new error messages, no abends, no nothing.

A co-worker recalls: "Physicists corrected a calculation for altitude, but our friend continued to doubt the results. The physicists said ridiculous. She fought them for two years. Finally she got hold of the program and checked it out. The correction subroutine was there, but unused. No program in the system called the correction routine; it had been marooned rather than installed."

Inventive ways to avoid actually testing new code include: assemblies run with NODECK preventing creation of a new object module, unchecked link-edits (which failed), or logic errors. Sometimes new code is inserted one card beyond where it should be — just after an unconditional branch, unreachable! Considerable time can be wasted incorrectly assuming that the change is installed.

When a change completely fails to function, explore the possibility, no matter how unlikely, that the new code was not, in fact, installed.

Absolute Patches

Since many of us program in assembler, patches developed using absolute modification techniques† are written in hexadecimal, octal, or binary strings, actually a language foreign to us. If a program that makes absolute modifications using assembler mnemonics is available, one source of patch errors, the manual translation from mnemonic to numeric operation code, can be avoided. When the patch becomes large, two dangers arise. There may be an error in the patch, unrelated to the problem we are working on or, when converting the patch from data to assembler language, a transcription error may then be introduced. (These dangers exist, of course, in a small patch, but the odds of making an error increase as the patch grows.)

When we replace a program that has been modified in absolute form with a fresh recompilation, we must first convert the absolute modification to a source language update or the patch will be lost in the shuffle. Recurrence of problems long since corrected is the irritating symptom here. As the number of absolute patches between recompilations grows, the odds of forgetting one also increase. Administrative controls, particularly automatic maintenance logging, can reduce, but not prevent, this problem.

I do not use a patch for a large correction unless it provides an evident major saving in time, for example, because the pro-

---

†On OS/360 and OS/VS systems, the utility used, and thus the practice itself, is called *super-zap*.

gram source is temporarily unavailable. (Better to work harder at having the source at hand.) Problems with patches are totally nonproductive and their resolution adds nothing to the quality of the program.

Hardware Monitor

A sophisticated form of hardware monitoring provides considerable help in improving software performance. The technique is akin to the Critical Path Method for project planning, but is performed once the system is operating.

Instruction Address Mapping

The hardware monitor is attached to the computer's instruction address field. When the address is within a predetermined range, the monitor develops a high-resolution frequency distribution of counts and addresses. A histogram is printed and compared against the software. We examine areas where many hits occur to improve CPU efficiency.

SAMPLE INSTRUCTION ADDRESS HISTOGRAM

ADDRESS	PERCENT	0-----10-----20-----30-----
00C5000-FF	0%	
00C5100-FF	10%	******
00C5200-FF	2%	*
00C5300-FF	1%	*
00C5400-FF	0%	
00C5500-FF	5%	****
00C5600-FF	30%	*********************
00C5700-FF	3%	**

Reviewing this plot, we can clearly see that the most promising area of the program to examine is between addresses C5600 and C56FF, as 30 percent of our time is spent there. Once we have examined that section of our program, we should proceed to the area between C5100 and C51FF, the 10 percent area.

Using the Monitor's Output

Once these bottlenecks, the innermost loops, are isolated, two general approaches occur. We can attempt to speed up the code segment by making specific changes within the "hot spot," or we can change program design to reduce the need to enter the routine. Naturally the latter approach offers the larger performance improvement, but potentially requires more sweeping changes. My preference is to start with a localized change, measure the improvement, and decide if further work is appropriate.

This technique reverses the coding practices of earlier days. Formerly, each instruction was written with considerable care, to save what time was possible. Today, we hunt for worthwhile places to improve efficiency. (I still write LA Rx,3(,Rx) instead of LA Rx,3(Rx) because on a 360/40 the first format is a machine cycle faster. So what? The 370/168 system I now use processes either as quickly.)

Difficulties

Problems with hardware monitoring abound. The monitoring is delicate. The monitor must be fast enough to capture the data, powerful enough to develop the histogram, and sensitive enough to avoid seriously reducing the voltages in the computer (thus causing hardware failures). The computer vendor's engineers will be lukewarm at best, because of the dangers to "their" machine. (Unconsciously the engineers may also fear equipment reductions. Oddly enough, system activity analysis, the most common use of a hardware monitor, usually results in a recommendation for more equipment, such as a larger central processor, more channels, more control units, more disks or drums!) Finally, some time must be taken to eliminate artifacts caused by incorrect monitor setup. My favorite, when monitoring instruction address data, is program activity reported in data buffers. On MVS systems, with multiple address spaces, the task is even tougher, as filtering by the protect key is needed to select the desired address space.

Software Monitors

A software monitor can often produce similar results, but for operating system software the performance implications of the monitor must themselves be measured. However, sometimes more subtle kinds of system interaction may be detected because the software monitor can correlate the contents of main storage with the instruction counter and thus tell more about system status.

The Payoff

The results are valuable. Hardware monitoring allowed us to modify a HASP system to reduce by a third the amount of CPU time it was consuming, a significant improvement in an already efficient package. The hardware monitor showed us that considerable time was spent in a particular HASP routine. Studying the routine, we realized that its function, searching a control block chain, could be done much faster. We reorganized the chain so that all control blocks of a particular type were contiguous and changed the routine to start searching at the first control block of the proper type, instead of the head of the chain. Once the control block type changed, we ended the search. Note that we had to change only one routine for this dramatic performance improvement.

We do not start optimizing before we find the bottleneck. Pareto's principle guides us here: 80 percent of the time is usually spent in 20 percent of the program. Only improvements to that 20 percent will have a dramatic effect on the program. We don't waste our time on the 80 percent of the code that doesn't matter much.

"Waste" a Little Machine Time

In solving a problem, don't be afraid to use some machine time to make the work easier. If you are looking for a text string buried in a module, have the machine search for it. If, with the proper breakpoints, an interactive test takes many minutes before the failing condition occurs, go ahead.

The economics of computing are that labor costs are sky-rocketing, while computer time is getting cheaper and cheaper by comparison. (A few years back, IBM reported that their software development costs had exceeded their hardware development costs for the first time. This undoubtedly reflects an industry trend.) If a bug can be resolved by an hour of careful desk checking, first investigate whether the same data might be available from a few minutes of computer time.

Vendor Support

Support is available for much of the software we use today. This major debugging resource takes the form of distributing maintenance updates, malfunction lists, and support personnel.

Maintenance

Vendor-supplied updates should be installed in a timely manner, once you have tested them thoroughly. Your goal should be to use the newest version the vendor has sent out, but to avoid being the *first* user of that new version.

Error Lists

When a malfunction occurs, review the list of known errors for the package. Sometimes the list will include your exact symptom, and an easy circumvention. Unfortunately a good imagination may be required to find the right bug on the list. If, for example, the failure is a program check, but is preceded by an error message, the bug list may only describe the problem as an error message or a program check but not both. A little detective work and a good imagination will help you read the malfunction list.

27

When you uncover a problem that appears to be caused by vendor-supplied software, take the time to fill out the appropriate forms to report the problem. Include as unequivocal a package of documentation as your time allows. A good error list does not appear by magic. Conscientious users reporting the problems they face make such lists possible. Even if the vendor is not enthusiastic about resolving errors, persist in your efforts: we report errors primarily to help fellow users, not the vendor.

Support Personnel

With few exceptions, the support people I have talked with are enthusiastic and knowledgeable about the products they support. Even if the problem is one that I have created, they are willing to give advice. That's the good news. Now for the bad.

A few are defensive and uncooperative. A more serious problem, however, is the vendor who places people between you and the competent support. Titles can be misleading here: "Technical Guru" may mask a blocker, rather than identify a helper. Fortunately initial impressions are usually accurate. If the person you are talking with doesn't immediately show a command of the software, he probably won't bloom in the course of a discussion. Look for a different helper. Persuade the Guru to put you in touch with the right person.

The three devices vendors may make available to you should all be exploited to help solve problems. Particularly with widely used programs and systems, many people will find the same difficulties you do and you can benefit from their experiences. Unfortunately the vendor cannot do everything; see the "User Group Meetings" chapter for another problem solving resource.

Automating the Arithmetic

Everyone has an electronic calculator these days. The Texas Instruments "Programmer" model is especially adapted for our needs. It adds, subtracts, multiplies, and divides in decimal, octal, and hexadecimal, and shifts in octal and hexadecimal.

The difference between studying a dump with and without a calculator in hand is phenomenal. Hexadecimal and octal arithmetic are serious enterprises for most of us, since we were raised in a base-ten world. Arithmetic can be a considerable distraction when working on a dump. Using the calculator, we spend less time on the arithmetic and more time on the logic. I realized hex calculators had arrived when I saw one on sale in a *department* store. No programmer examining a dump should be without one.

Sometimes debugging will require a calculation that is cumbersome even with the calculator. Conversion between various formats of disk record addresses comes to mind. The calculations, consisting of several multiplications, divisions, and remainderings, have no educational value once the technique is learned.

I write small routines (in FORTRAN) to automate these functions. The computer can do the conversion more easily than I can by hand. Furthermore the result will be correct. Interactive debuggers can often perform similar conversions, including complicated ones such as interpreting floating-point data. A programmable calculator can also perform these computations.

The specialized hand calculator and interactive conversion routines allow us to spend less time on arithmetic and more on debugging. Equip yourself with both these tools.

Enqueue Lockouts

The *deadly embrace* is an expensive system failure. By actual timing, an experienced computer operator may take between a half hour and an hour to recognize and act on the condition. During that time, the system responds to operator queries, masking the stoppage, but does not process any work. We are behooved to resolve lockout problems quickly.

The theoretical paradigm is as follows: task 1 requests resource A, task 2 requests resource B, task 1 waits for resource B (currently held by task 2), and, the crucial event, task 2 waits for resource A (currently held by task 1). Deadlock! One task must be cancelled for processing to resume.

Nothing fundamental in OS/360 or OS/VS prevents enqueue lockouts. That OS/360 and OS/VS systems are not constantly hung in enqueue lockouts is due to a standard protocol for using the facility:† the rich facilities of the system include no protection against the condition. Fortunately, enqueue lockouts, in my experience, are fairly rare.

Implied enqueues, not accomplished by the ENQ SVC, further complicate matters. One example comes readily to mind: in SVS and MVT, the TSO function that locks the TSO session into its region of memory. Since this locking-in effectively locks

---

†J. W. Havender, "Avoiding Deadlock in Multitasking Systems," *IBM Systems Journal* 7, no. 2 (1968), pp. 74–84, discusses the protocol. The approaches used are reprinted in Appendix A. Richard C. Holt, "Some Deadlock Properties of Computer Systems," *Computer Surveys* 4, no. 3 (September 1972), 179–196 presents formal techniques for detecting potential deadlocks in computer systems.

the other sessions out of the region, in effect the session enqueues itself *ahead* of other sessions using the region.

What to Look For

The first step to resolving a lockout is to explain it. In OS or OS/VS, a formatted listing (trace) of the queue control blocks (QCBs) allows one to determine which tasks are at the tops of the various queues. Once the tasks at the tops of the various queues are found, determine which of these tasks is ahead of the others. All but one task will appear in other queues, in subordinate positions. This task is holding up system processing.

Once the top task in all queues is located, one must determine why that task is not processing: what event would start it? Again, a formatted dump is most helpful, since that task must be examined in detail.

Simple Example

When a communications task runs out of message buffers, it uses standard message handling routines (in effect, calling on itself) to report the problem to the operator. The condition immediately becomes permanent, because only the communications task can free up buffers.

Longer Example

One failure I resolved occurred only during heavy use of SMF accounting. SMF could not write records as fast as they were queued. TSO session "A" would attempt to queue an accounting record, be put into wait state and swapped out of its region. A local modification to the HASP system would attempt to queue an accounting record, and also be put into wait state, behind TSO session "A." TSO session "B," now in the swapping region formerly occupied by "A," would set up a request to HASP to return some job output, lock itself into the region (a requirement of our interface), post HASP, and wait for the output. At that moment, the system was deadlocked.

The QCB trace showed an SMF queue with many users stacked on it:

SAMPLE QCB TRACE FROM ENQUEUE LOCKOUT PROBLEM

```
MAJOR 2360C0    NAME SYSSMF01

    MINOR 236120  NAME BUF
         . . . . . . . . . . . . . . SESSION "A" . . . . . . . .
         . . .
         . . .(other tasks between HASP and SESSION "A")
         . . .
         . . . . . . . . . . . . . . TASK HASP   . . . . . . . .
```

TSO user "A" was first, and the HASP system was lower in the queue. Only by reviewing the dump did it become clear that TSO user "A" could not continue. The SMF backup and wait had long been satisfied, but the swap region was now unavailable.

To Summarize

TSO session "A" waits for SMF, HASP waits for SMF, TSO session "B" locks itself into "A"'s region, and waits for HASP.

This problem could have been resolved by either eliminating the TSO request to lock the region in memory, or moving the HASP SMF request to a subtask, allowing the main HASP task to forge ahead during heavy SMF use. We took the first action.

When IBM implemented HASP use of SMF, they took the second action, preventing similar problems.

Only with careful planning can we avoid enqueue problems. The techniques discussed in Appendix A will guide you to program designs that prevent lockouts.

Reading Code

Just as proofreading the written word is an effective way to detect errors, proofreading a program can uncover many errors. Don't neglect this technique. You can read code any time of day or night, and since no computer is required, you can do so anywhere.

When I first started programming, the system I used had turnaround of about two to three runs per day. Because I could not afford to waste a turnaround on typos, I soon learned the syntax of FORTRAN, the language I was coding in. Fortunately there was a card listing machine available, with nearly instant turnaround, so that clean listings were readily available.

Almost any sort of error can be found by reading code. Some errors can most easily be detected from the listing. Marking branches and loops can further illuminate the code. I use a felt-tip marker to mark edges of pages where I want to return and reread the code or where bugs or sloppy code have been found. This speeds up locating the right page in an inch-thick listing.

A checklist can help focus attention on particularly error prone practices. My list for assembler language programs appears in Appendix B.

Although the machine can help us in any number of ways, proofreading a program always improves our understanding of it and frequently will lead us to a hitherto undetected problem. Most terminals, including display tubes with screen splitting and selective exclusion, offer a very narrow window through which to view a program; paper listings present more information. We come away from reading listings with a far better grasp of our program than the terminal affords us.

Did You Use the Same Model Throughout?

Sometimes, you must modify a program to change the data representation whenever it appears. A field formerly one-byte wide might become a fullword, a binary field might assume decimal representation. When reading the code, the old format will look right if you don't constantly remind yourself that a new format is in use. Thorough debugging can be slow work because the probability of error is high.

When reading the code, try a sweep for consistency. Start with the cross-reference listing and follow the use of each reformatted variable through the program. Alternately, do a search with the text editor to find every occurrence of the variables you have changed.

Consider changing the name of the field. This will produce an immediate alarm from the assembler or compiler when an old format usage is encountered. Further, future systems programmers, whether examining the code using outdated system documentation or attempting to install a modification developed elsewhere, will be alerted to the format change automatically.

In general, use extra caution with a data representation change, as a 95 percent conversion to the new format is unacceptable.

Timing Problems

AXIOM: For any two unsynchronized processes, conditions exist such that the slower one will sometimes outrace the faster one!

I went through a period of relying on relative speeds of processes to remain the same regardless of system load, hardware reliability, device or CPU speed, and wind velocity. Each time I eventually learned otherwise.

The pattern was very predictable. The code would test beautifully, even under fairly heavy test loads. Production operation of the software would look good, too. Weeks would pass, occasionally months, but eventually problems would arise. Symptoms tended to be peculiar to the circumstances: in one case, a program check would occur, in another, a job would become "stuck" in the system. Something would throw the timing off: hardware problems on a disk pack, heavy load through the timing dependent path, or a new device or central processing unit with different timing characteristics.

Now my rule is: Never count on one process outracing another; always determine that the first ended. Synchronization controls must be coded and tested to eliminate timing dependencies.

It Must Be Hardware!

Breathes there a systems programmer with a heart so dead as never to have said, "the machine must be broken."† Blaming the equipment is an attractive approach, partly because few of us fully understand the computer's inner workings. In the early days of computing, vacuum-tube machines did show poor reliability. Today's systems are worlds better. Unfortunately we must do more than point fingers if we wish to improve system reliability. The notes that follow should help you recognize the signs of failing hardware so that you and the engineers can cooperate in returning the machine to service.

System failures fall into four categories:

---

†My thanks to Robert Johnson of Boeing Computer Services Company for his comments and suggestions on this chapter.

1. Software failures, which systems programmers correct by replacing incorrect code.
2. Hardware failures, which the engineers correct by replacing failing components of the computer.
3. Hardware-induced software failures (the software fails trying to recover from a hardware problem), which both the systems programmers and the engineers each separately correct as in (1) and (2).
4. Hardware failures that do not disclose themselves as such.

This last area requires that systems programmers work with the engineers to find the problem.

An Uneasy Situation

On each side, a natural reaction is to throw up one's hands and announce that the difficulties in the other party's area of expertise are causing the problem. Simply finding a technical vocabulary common between hardware engineers and systems programmers can be difficult. In systems implemented with read-only storage, the hardware registers may differ from the programming registers. On the 360/65, programmers spoke of registers 1 through 16, while the engineers spoke of registers A, B, X, and Y. Since failures that require such cooperation are rare, the engineers and the systems programmers do not have many opportunities to work together. This class of failures cannot be diagnosed quickly, and as time passes both the engineers and the systems programmers are under a good deal of management pressure to solve the problem. Finally, the hardware diagnostics did not show that anything was wrong.

What to Do

First, make sure that all the hardware diagnostics have been run. Usually computer manufacturers prepare a variety of diagnostic programs for their systems. We have not exhausted all hope of the diagnostics turning up the error, of course, until they all have been run. (In the situation described in "Special Instruction Sets," only the decimal instruction diagnostics showed any failure. If the engineer had not run those tests, the hardware failure would have not been disclosed.) Remember that once a system has been down for several hours, allowing the engineers to take two hours to run *all* the diagnostics will not significantly increase the system outage, and might move you closer to the problem. Ensure that your engineers have the best possible diagnostics at hand. Sometimes area or regional specialists have special diagnostic programs not used by the local engineers. Cooperate with the engineers in any way you can and ask about additional support from specialists.

Doing Your Part

In addition to supporting and encouraging the engineers, you should attempt to isolate the problem yourself. When reviewing a failure, attempt to define the *first* problem encountered as accurately as possible. Sometimes this description will suggest that a hardware failure caused the problem. Here are some typical symptoms:

- *Memory Symptoms.*   Memory failures often show one of two patterns, depending on which component failed. A cell of memory may go bad and return incorrect information. On older, non-virtual memories, diagnosis was pretty easy, since the same memory address would be implicated. On today's virtual machines, however, different virtual addresses, mapped to the same real address at different times, suffer the failure. When cells of virtual memory change inexplicably, calculate and compare the real addresses of the failing cells.

    The hardware that reads and writes storage may also malfunction. In these failures, a specific bit of the memory access field will be set or cleared (picked or dropped, in hardware parlance). For example, if the machine accesses memory in single bytes, a specific bit in any byte in memory may be altered. Similarly, if the machine accesses memory in doublewords, a specific bit in any doubleword in memory may be altered.

- *Instruction Set Symptoms.* Specific instructions in the system may fail. (Again, see "Special Instruction Sets.") Sometimes they fail in relatively obvious ways, so that the instruction *always* returns incorrect results. However, timing may be involved; the instruction only fails when certain other conditions are satisfied. For example, the instruction works properly unless input/output to the disk is in progress.

- *Device Symptoms.* Failures specific to input/output devices may show a wider range of symptoms than the preceding problems. The failure may be reflected on the device media, or in the computer.

  At one installation, where accounting information was punched on cards, I often spoke with the accounting staff and the engineers about invalid punched output. The accounting staff assured me that the bad accounting cards, multi-punched, off-punched, or even shifted data on the card reflected software problems. I was flattered by their belief in my skills, but when I asked the engineer about this, he assured me that even the shifted data on the cards was probably a device problem.

  When a paging disk or drum becomes ill, the first signs of trouble may be program checks experienced by the system's users. The paging device brings in mangled data, or perhaps strings of zeros, which the computer cannot execute as instructions.

  Practically everyone who has used a minicomputer to simulate a teleprocessing front-end has learned that, although OS/360 may ask for six bytes of sense information, it really only has room for one, and if more bytes are returned, disaster strikes. Unit control blocks suffer damage from the overlay by the front-end.

Taking the Offensive

After a few failures, we can attempt to beat the hardware diagnostic programmers at their own game. A friend describes his experiences writing his own diagnostic routine: "We were suffering unexplained memory protection violations. We changed disk packs, went to backup versions of the operating system, everything we could think of and the failures continued. Finally, I wrote a simple stand-alone test routine. For each 2K block of memory, I ran the block's protect key and my program protect key from zero to 15, storing into the block using each key setting. I then moved to the next block, and did the same test. Once the program had tested all of memory this way, it started over. I hit pay dirt almost immediately, and the hardware engineers were able to quickly isolate and resolve the formerly intermittent problem.''

"I keyed the original version of the program into memory by hand, but I have since located a stand-alone loader routine, and I now have a version I can assemble under the operating system and load from cards or tape. I've used it a couple of times since, and I keep it handy just in case."

Hardware failures often require many recurrences before a pattern can be deduced. Patience and good recordkeeping are important in resolving hardware difficulties, particularly if they are intermittent or esoteric. Additionally, two investments of your time will pay large dividends when elusive hardware problems occur. First, take time to learn to write your own diagnostics, as described earlier. Such learning activities are much easier if you are not under pressure to produce results. Second, make friends with the engineers responsible for your system. If your day-to-day relations with them are comfortable, then cooperation under pressure is much more likely. Don't be afraid to lend them a hand when you can.

Save Area Mismanagement

When I moved from using an IBM 7040, equipped with three
index registers, an accumulator, and a multiplier/quotient register, to the System/360, equipped with sixteen general-purpose
registers, I expected register saving to be less trouble. I learned
that we must protect register contents carefully regardless of the
computer we are using. Three major techniques protect registers.

Managed Save Areas

Standard save areas are allocated and freed as modules are entered and exited. (See the example under "Reentrancy.")

Problem to Expect: Running out of Memory

If a module fails to free its save area on exit, all of memory will
eventually be filled with save areas, and the program will fail.
Recursively entered modules can cause this by failing to return
after recursion is complete. Operating system exits, which generally allocate a save area when first entered, must save a pointer
to the allocated area. Otherwise the exit will repeatedly allocate
a save area, consuming all of memory.

Hidey Hole Save Areas

Within a module, presumably to save time or storage, shortcut context saving is used: only a few registers are saved, in a separate area. (The module usually has a save area, but internally the shortcut method is used.)

Problem to Expect: Loops

As modifications are installed, the shortcut save areas become more and more heavily used. Accidental duplicate use of a specific shortcut area results in a second-level return address stored on top of the first-level return address. The first-level routine will then continuously return to itself.

Limited Depth Save Areas

The system supports a specific, limited number of save areas. (Exactly three, for example.)

Problem to Expect: Running out of Areas

As the system grows, a case will develop in which the specific number of save areas is not enough. "If I try to do a LIST under BATCH, the system says SAVE AREA DEPTH EXCEEDED." (Frequently, we solve problems with limited depth save areas using hidey hole save areas.)

When designing a new system, managed save areas should be the technique of choice. A system built on them will not face future limits of function implicit in the other two techniques. Remember our performance improvement technique: don't optimize until you must. When correcting problems with existing systems, the temptation to reuse normally unused data areas should be resisted. You face fewer dangers from adding a hidey hole than from borrowing someone else's.

Loops

Looping under program control is an important programming technique. An understanding of the four elements of a loop will allow us to appreciate what can go wrong within the loop. The elements are:

- INITIALIZE (the counter)
- PROCESSING (the data)
- MODIFICATION (of the counter)
- TEST (for loop completion)

Initialize

Not much of this, is there? Consider the following FORTRAN segment:

```
            M=6
            N=5
            DO 100 I=M,N
            ... other code
   100      CONTINUE
```

FORTRAN has always had the quirk that DO loops execute once before loop conditions are tested, so that even though the starting value, M, at 6, exceeds the termination value, N, at 5,

"other code" will be entered once. We probably are not programming in FORTRAN, but particularly in assembler languages,
special care must be taken to ensure that guaranteed one pass
loops are not accidentally coded.

Processing

Perhaps the most common error in the processing part of a loop
is the "off by one" error: if the counter runs from 1 to N and
data elements are to be referenced with the counter, we could
miss the first element if we don't compensate for starting at 1.

Modification

Incrementing or decrementing the loop counter.

Test

Determining that no further processing is required. Various sorts
of problems can cause our test, if it goes beyond a simple compare, to fail. Mathematical formulas, requiring repeated evaluation, don't always converge in our fixed-width registers. Even
if we know our error, E, will be less than .001 after five iterations
(certainly this happened in each of the dozen test cases), the
loop should be tested for completion both by checking E and
by counting passes to prevent a runaway. Continuing along this
thread, another FORTRAN segment:

```
      DO 100 I=2,10
      ... (computation)
      IF (A.LT.B) GO TO 200
100   CONTINUE
200   WRITE(6,30) A
```

The user may want to know if our loop found what we were looking for, or if we simply terminated at $I = 10$. The preceding code treats these two cases identically. Better to have at least issued a warning between statements 100 and 200.

Another form of "off by one" error can creep into the TEST part of the loop. If the data element has N items, you may count from 1 to N, or count from 0 to $N - 1$, but *not* count from 0 to N. Processing 0 to N will process one too many elements, with the associated danger of invalid results or overlaid data.

When coding or examining loops, remember the four elements and the associated dangers and you will be alert to error prevention and discovery.

Follow-up

1. Using "Special Debugging Tools" and your own system's documentation, make a list of the debugging tools available on your system. Now indicate the frequency with which you use each tool. If you find tools you never use, try them out on an invented problem, so that you will be more tempted to invoke them when you need them.

2. Design, code, and install "Instrumentation" into a software system you work on.

3. Make a list of complicated calculations you normally perform manually and develop an automated method, either selected from "Automating the Arithmetic" or your own design, to simplify the process.

4. Take a program of your own, or borrow one from a co-worker, and, using the checklist in Appendix B, conduct a "Reading Code" exercise.

SECTION 2

Operating Procedures and Tools

Every computer installation develops operator procedures (formal or informal) and collects information about its operation. Flaws in these areas can seriously hurt system reliability. Weaknesses in operating procedures can lose valuable time and information, while poor data collection or preservation sacrifices a valuable debugging resource.

System reliability sits on a foundation of certain production runs and standards of machine operation. Accounting data, system console information, and operator procedures combine to form the concrete of our foundation. For problems that require it, methodically collected and preserved information is irreplaceable.

Once the data are stored, tools are needed to use them: extract routines and suitable equipment complete the foundation. The following topics will show you how to collect and use the data you need.

Clean Dumps

Solving problems requires clean dumps. Allowing random agitation of the system by operator commands, readying disk drives, or canceling jobs may or may not clear up the condition, but are guaranteed to muddy the waters for the troubleshooter who must solve the problem. A clear log of these actions is usually unavailable, and the actions themselves can destroy valuable data in the dump. The temptation to be a hero and get the system moving again is strong, but succumbing can prevent permanent resolution of the original difficulty.

With applications programs, losing data is less common. However, the dump program, if entered without sufficient memory, overlays allocated memory before writing the dump out. The overlay seriously hurts your chances of getting a usable dump. Padding your original memory request can eliminate needless reruns to get a clean dump.

Console Message Logs

Frequently, system errors and failures are preceded by messages issued to the operator console. If we routinely save the console log, we can examine these messages long after the problem occurs.

Console messages are a controversial topic. The most extreme position I know belongs to a chap who says, "All informational messages are a waste of the operator's time and attention. Issue only action messages; let queries replace informational messages." I allow the system to issue the full complement of messages, but write many of them only to the log on disk. They never go to a console. By including all system messages on the log, much more data is available for problem resolution.

Post-processors write the log to tape and microfiche, and prepare reports. When I first implemented the support, the reports included only a sequential listing of the messages and a listing sorted by job number. As time passed, co-workers added perhaps a half dozen other reports. One summarized disk and tape mounts, another listed all security messages. Console messages are informative, if they can be filtered and organized. Microfiche improves matters further, because orderly storage of fiche cards is much more likely than orderly storage of foot-thick listings.

Folks resolving system problems quickly beat a path to the console logs because of the wealth of information they provide.

Maintenance and Failure Logs

To solve some problems, we must reconstruct and compare the histories of software changes and failures. For major changes, like a new release of the operating system, such information is usually retained. Resolving problems with smaller changes often requires knowing when they were installed, just as with more dramatic changes. Unfortunately, without methodic practices, this information can easily be lost.

Who can remember if our troubles, which began, say, three months ago, preceded or followed the newly added feature. If we know for sure that they followed the new feature, we have a good place to look.

Poor logging is usually more common on smaller systems. The bureaucracy associated with the larger machines has some benefit in this area. Automated logging of maintenance by the system software can be helpful, but is only part of the solution. Disciplined personnel willing to log even the small changes are required.

Develop a tracking system for your modifications. Assign each one an identifier, alphabetic or numeric, and note when you install the change. Mark the modification itself, as described in the "Comments in Assembler Language" chapter. Track failures the same way; assign a number to each and log them. I have seen manual systems based on sheets in a notebook, semiautomatic systems using a data file stored on the computer, and such fully automatic systems as IBM's SMP† satisfy the need. I recommend that you use whichever technique is most readily available to you.

---

†*OS/VS System Modification Program (SMP) System Programmer's Guide*, IBM, form C28–0673.

No One Else Has Reported This Problem

Sensitive handling of problem reports will allow you to resolve system problems in a timely fashion.

Once, when I worked for a consulting firm, we were normally the only users of the system's magnetic tape drives. We had considerable trouble with them and regularly reported problems to our customer, the owner of the machine, who informed us that no one else had complained. We arrived one day, and the drives were being torn apart by maintenance engineers. Our customer had written six weeks' work onto one of the drives and lost everything! Revenge was not particularly sweet. We needed the repairs long before. Our customer's substantial loss to the equipment didn't benefit us.

Three morals arise from this episode:

1. When reporting problems, don't accept the "no one but you has this trouble" song. Insist that your problem, however unique, be treated seriously.

2. When handling complaints, don't ignore the first signs of a potentially major problem, simply because only a few first signs are observed. Investigate the difficulty, try to replicate it, and then correct it.

3. If you wait long enough, a problem that didn't seem important will hurt you.

Extract Routines

Once procedures are in place to salt away information about the operating environment, routines must be available to extract and present that information.

When studying a system problem, you may want, from either accounting (SMF) or console (SYSLOG) data tapes, information for a particular time range during a day or for a particular job. (The failure that interests you may be associated with either a certain time frame or a specific job. You can more easily resolve a problem associated with a particular job, for example, if messages and accounting records peculiar to that job can be brought together, with unrelated noise stripped away.) Additionally, special kinds of records may be desired from the accounting tape (selected by record type) and the console tape (selected by message number).

Generalized extract routines do not represent a particularly serious programming challenge; if you have not already acquired or developed your own, go ahead and write the ones you need. They will quickly pay for themselves in speeding your work.

Peripheral Power

Project managers generally understand that computer time is required to produce computer programs. Unfortunately this understanding has not uniformly spread to cover the hardware required for software development. The most frustrating debugging I ever did was on a minicomputer equipped with only a teletype. Many of the techniques and tools that I use rely on peripherals that support high data rates. Working on a machine without these devices can be humbling. Outdated program listings make debugging a game of blind man's buff.

Although larger systems usually have high-performance peripherals to match, poor equipment often characterizes the smaller machine. Choose devices powerful enough to support the job a mini- or microcomputer will do. On a production system, a fast hardcopy device, for example, may not be needed but on a development system it usually is. High-speed peripherals, tapes and disks, hasten development. ("God fights on the side with the heavy artillery.") Peripherals may be available through a fast data link to another system rather than dedicated to your system. The key issues are data rate and turnaround rather than physical attachment.

Slow equipment will increase development time and reduce programmer efficiency. Remember, equipment prices are dropping, while salaries are rising out of sight. At today's prices, a device that rents for $100 a month pays for itself when saving about a half of a person-day's work a month, or about twelve person-minutes per day. (See Appendix C for more about systems programmer costs.) A simple time-motion study will show you how easily a slow device can cause a twelve-minute-a-day delay. Shorting the equipment doesn't cut costs if personnel productivity is sacrificed.

Review the equipment available for your environment regularly and, if better hardware tools would speed your work, ask for them.

Better Terminals

Pay some attention to the tools you use. Hundreds of people, working for dozens of companies, have spent considerable time developing better terminals. The improvements have been sweeping: the terminals are not only more reliable and sometimes less expensive, but also support faster transfer rates and wider output lines.

Once, terminal speeds of 10 to 15 character per second (cps) were standard, and the newer 30-cps machines were thought supersonic. Times have changed. The industry standard for hard-copy terminals is 30 characters per second, and machines that operate at 120 cps are used routinely. For video terminals, speeds up to 960 cps are in general use.

Surprisingly, the human eye rapidly adapts to higher speeds, and the brain learns to absorb information faster. Investigate higher data rates; they will improve your productivity dramatically because you will spend less time waiting for the computer.

When using batch- and line-printer-oriented programs from a terminal, the output is much more readable if the terminal line width matches that assumed by the program.

Many terminals presently on the market offer platens or screens between 72 and 80 characters wide. Most of the batch programs around assume line printer output, and produce print lines between 120 and 132 characters long. Terminal systems offer a variety of methods to handle the discrepancy: some simply print the line as two lines on the terminal, some truncate the line at terminal width, and still others shorten strings of blanks in the output to make the line fit. Unfortunately none of these methods is completely satisfactory.

You don't have to live with narrow terminals. Many manufacturers offer hardcopy terminals with platens 132 positions wide (or wider) supporting line speeds up to 120 characters per second. At this writing, the Datagraphix 132A and 132B terminals, the Datamedia DT 80/1, and the Digital Equipment VT100 terminal are readily available, 132-character-wide, video terminals. Switching to the wider output line instantly makes batch program output more intelligible.

The terminal market changes even more rapidly than the mainframe market: if you are using the same terminal you used four years ago, a better terminal is probably available. You should periodically review the market to see if you can find a better tool for your work.

Home Terminals

The economics of the computing industry have shifted so much that a natural management decision is to provide home terminals to every systems programmer who wishes one. Despite this shift, the home terminal is not yet universal. Let us review the arguments for and against the home terminal.

First, let's work out the economics of the terminal. A 120-character-per-second display terminal, including coupler, costs around $100 a month, $1200 a year, or 2½ percent of the cost, to the company, of the systems programmer ($48,000). (See the figures and discussion in Appendix C.) If having the home terminal persuades the programmer to put in 2½ percent more work (50 hours a year, slightly over four hours a month, one hour a week), the terminal has paid for itself.

The home terminal offers some additional benefits. Having

systems programmers using the system whenever it is available can provide them with a strong incentive to improve system performance and reliability. Of more immediacy, some kinds of systems problems can be circumvented by the programmer using the terminal from home. Although our emphasis throughout this book is on problem prevention and elimination, in a pinch, diagnosis and workaround using a terminal from home is faster than waiting for the staffer to drive in. Further, a system crash may be averted this way.

In situations where the office environment is more interruption-prone than the home, program development using the home terminal can be considerably quicker. With rising gasoline prices, more programmers may find this attractive. Also, time lost situations caused by programmers staying home and waiting for appliance repairs, for example, can be reduced. The benefit to the company appears in reduced flow time for the work.

Some managers may be uncomfortable having staff members at work but out of sight. Oddly enough, few of these same managers insist on being present for the midnight-to-dawn machine shots we often have to use. Over the shoulder supervision is more a need of the manager than the programming task. Certainly some aspects of the systems programmer's job require face-to-face meetings with others, but some facets of the work do not.

Other supervisors are deathly afraid that systems programmers will spend all their time playing computer games rather than working. One would hope that the supervisor could detect this directly from the individual's productivity, without having to rely on inspection of terminal sessions. Certainly, during evening hours, when computers are usually less loaded, the "lost" computing time involved would have been lost anyway. No one has yet discovered a method of storing computer time for later use. It must be consumed immediately.

Once you get the home terminal idea across, a bright manager may suggest, as a cost-savings measure, that instead of each staffer having his own terminal, a "pool" of terminals should be shared among the staffers. Resist this idea.

In the environment where I saw "pooled" terminals in action, several bad things happened:

1. Since no individual was responsible for any particular terminal, all the pool terminals were in poor condition. Mal-

functions were never repaired, because no one took responsibility for the terminal.

2. The "pool" concept suggests a stack of terminals in the manager's office, ready to be checked out. That was true for about the first week, but then most of the terminals migrated to people's houses and stayed there. To use a "pool" terminal, one had to find out who had one, and persuade him to bring it in. Tomorrow. If they don't forget. Spontaneous home use of the computer by the have-nots was eliminated.

3. Tracking of the pool terminals was also very difficult. Disputes erupted over whether a particular terminal at the office belonged to one individual or to the "pool." To some extent, marking the terminals would help, but once the terminal has left the office, the best markings in the world are invisible.

The extra aggravation of pooled terminals is not worth the supposed cost savings, particularly because individual home terminals are cost effective in their own right. If home terminals are not available to you, start lobbying for them.

Manuals

If knowledge is power, then our manuals are one of our most important tools. When we choose to have a personal copy of a manual, we are making decisions about our time, what we spend on manuals, and use of our shelf space, all finite resources.

What to Have

I keep personal copies of every manual I refer to as often as once a month. I also have copies of specific manuals I use perhaps only once a year, but intensely for a short period during the year. The economics of owning a manual are relatively simple: our hypothetical systems programmer (see Appendix C for more about systems programmer costs) spends the price of a $4 manual in ten minutes time finding one to borrow. The ten minutes might be divided into three searches of just over three minutes each. However, in addition to shelf space, there is another hidden cost: updating.

Updates

As software and hardware changes, new editions of manuals appear. That's good, because you can usually simply throw the old manual away. Unfortunately, sometimes more minor changes are reflected in revisions to existing manuals: an update of between two pages and 75 percent of the original manual is distributed. When such an update arrives, I don't automatically drop everything and start installing the update. Manual updating is slow, boring work. Before I forge ahead, I first determine whether the update corresponds to a level of the system we have. If it describes features we haven't yet installed, I defer updating. Then I determine if the manual is one I am using every day. If not, I again set the update aside. This practice isn't laziness, but good time management. Frequently I can wait out a major update to a manual I don't use very often and pick up a completely new edition, saving for all time the cost of that updating.

"Current" Manuals

As systems programmers, we seem doomed to having two copies of many of our manuals, one for the production system, and one for the new system we are working towards installing. Throughout my career I have had to keep copies of two different editions of at least one, but usually several, manuals. This fact must be considered when determining how much shelf space we require.

Learning of New Manuals

Larger installations employ a librarian who keeps up with manual revisions and orders what is needed. Some suppliers offer automatic revision distribution. Neither of these services, however, completely replaces you knowing the literature: it pays to periodically review the supplier's catalog and the "related publications" list at the front of your manuals. Manuals are sometimes split into two new manuals, or the reverse, two manuals are merged into one new one, and you cannot always rely on support systems to handle this.

How to Use Manuals

Frequently, once you have read and mastered a manual, you will find yourself constantly hunting for a particular chart. I attach a paperclip or stick-on flap to such key pages and eliminate flipping through the book. Don't be afraid to write notes on your manuals, but remember that the next edition will require that you transcribe your notes.

System Logic Manuals

Reading logic manuals is a special skill. When installing OS/SVS and HASP 4.0, we decided that the HASP region had to be addressable by user jobs in the system. Initial attempts to read data in the region met with protection violations. A quick study of the problem showed that in the virtual storage "user segment table," (associated with user jobs), the HASP region was marked as inaccessible. A simple change corrected that, but tests still showed that the memory was protected from access by user jobs! Careful study of the dump showed minute differences: instead of a segment table exception, we faced a fetch protection exception. A routine to simply turn off the fetch protect bits in the HASP region might not resolve the problem, since the paging supervisor might remove and replace some of the HASP memory without respecting the flag. In fact, the routine might encounter parts of the region that weren't swapped in. My partner in crime for this project reviewed the page supervisor logic manual and discovered a software extension to the hardware page tables in which protect key information was stored, and was able to write a change that covered all cases.

Reporting Errors

Manuals, even ones we write ourselves, are never perfect. Sometimes, they aren't even right! When we discover problems with a manual, we owe it to the writer, as well as fellow readers, to point out the problems, in writing, to the supplier. Such letters are always read and usually acted on.

Manuals are our tools. We need an appropriate collection of documents, current for the software we are using, at our fingertips. We must do some planning to make that collection a reality.

Follow-up

1. Follow up on "Maintenance and Failure Logs" by reviewing the logging techniques your installation currently uses, and determining what problems exist and how the logging could be improved.

2. Develop one or more "Extract Routines" to fill real needs at your shop.

3. After reading "Better Terminals" and "Home Terminals," talk to a terminal salesman to find out what terminals are now available, what they cost, and what they can do for you that your current equipment cannot. If you find a machine that is better than anything you now have, prepare a proposal for your management to replace or augment existing equipment with what you have found.

SECTION 3

Prevention

In the "Debugging" section, the focus was on getting out of a mess, rather than preventing one. Although we spend a good deal of our time debugging and correcting, we may exchange debugging time for development time. Where possible, these exchanges should be made. Development time (design and coding) is fairly predictable; milestones may be scheduled and tracked. Debugging and testing time can be unpredictable, and are certainly a large part of the programming development effort. The preventions should take less time than the debugging time required by their absence.

This section emphasizes preventing problems through planning and design. The following section focuses on coding techniques, particularly in assembler language, that also prevent program errors.

Structured Walkthroughs

Good programmers have discussed their work informally for years. Such discussions improve the work being done, and should be encouraged. Better still, we can formalize such discussions and improve them further.†

At a structured walkthrough, one technician describes the program, what it does, how it works, all in considerable detail. Other technicians listen carefully, and attempt to understand the function as well as possible. They ask questions to expose possible weak points in the design. Sometimes, in the course of preparing or delivering the exposition, the presenter will have insights about the code. The technique has not then failed, but has succeeded in another way.

The benefits to the preparer are not new. Years ago, a friend of mine sometimes would say, "Let me explain this problem I have to you." We would sit down, and he would describe the situation carefully to me, and I would listen attentively, occasionally asking questions. Usually, about halfway through his explanation, he would announce, "Oh, darn!" Victory! I liked his results so well I tried it myself, with equally great success. We sometimes wondered if a tape player with a loop saying, "uhuh" would have done as well as the listener. I later learned the answer: one company purchased a life-sized dummy, named him Joe, and seated him in a conference room. Staffers

†For further discussion of reviews, see Daniel P. Freedman and Gerald M. Weinberg, *The EthnoTECHnical Review Handbook,* 2d. ed. (Lincoln, Neb.: Ethnotech, 1979), available from Ethnotech, Inc., P.O. Box 6627, Lincoln, NB 68506.

would sit down and explain their problems to Joe with much the same results we experienced.

The presence of supervisory personnel can turn the cooperative effort of seeking the truth into a fault-finding mission with the presenter trying to cover his tail, while the listeners try to score points. To avoid introducing a conflict of interest into the walkthrough, resist the temptation to invite supervisors of other participants to your walkthroughs.

Although many sources speak of the structured walkthrough as a design tool, we can use it at any phase of a programming project. If the code exists, so much the better, as questions about details of the implementation can be pursued directly. Some sources call this sort of walkthrough a code *inspection*. If we have only a design, and no program, the walkthrough can prepare us to code.

Plan for Debugging

Obviously, every program will require debugging. Just as obviously, debugging may be easy or hard. Given the choice, select the easy ways.

For example, on a system with TSO (or any terminal system that allows interactive testing), the rewards for developing a function using TSO are considerable. A 2000-line program tested with a debugger will usually become operational sooner than a 100-line SVC. The delays involved in waiting to try the next reassembly of the SVC are murder. If, instead of developing a new SVC for your project, you can use an existing one, the savings in debugging time will be dramatic, even if it takes more code to use the existing SVC.

I developed an initialization module for a WYLBUR®† system that eliminated the need for DD statements to define the disks WYLBUR would use. Although in production the module runs as a WYLBUR "subsystem," it was first coded and tested as a program run under TSO. Once the functions that could be TESTed under TSO were working correctly, minor modifications converted it to run under WYLBUR. Debugging would have taken considerably longer had I started out testing it as a WYLBUR subsystem.

I isolated those functions that could run independently of the larger system (WYLBUR) they would ultimately reside in, and coded and tested them separately. Dummy interfaces can facilitate this sort of testing.

---

†WYLBUR is a registered trademark of the Trustees of Stanford University.

You can take this one step further. In designing software, make choices for easier debugging. Consider data representation. *Eyecatchers,* characters format fields within program code and data areas are most helpful when examining storage, regardless of whether a dump or a debugger is in use. Similarly, you may choose to store key data items in control blocks in a storage inefficient format so that you can interpret them more easily when debugging.

Various authorities report that around half of our programming time is spent debugging. Given this staggering percentage, we owe it to ourselves to devise methods to make the debugging faster and easier. Program design should include debugging considerations.

Avoiding Yesterday's Efficiency

In the early days of System/360, good system performance required keeping the operating system small. Many of us developed habits that linger on, despite the change in direction: memory isn't so important now, and on larger systems, where a second is divided into over a million instruction executions, CPU time isn't critical, either. (The 370/168 I use today is roughly 28 times faster than the 360/40 I once used.)

A few years ago, I spent weeks developing a resource manager. A key feature of the manager was that all the resource counts — memory, tapes, and disks — fit quite snugly into a single word (32 bits) of memory. I developed half-byte counters especially for the occasion.

The half-byte counters were a great deal of trouble to implement, reduced the generality of the code involved, and required an untimely rework. (Half-byte means a limit of 15 for the count. Our sixteenth tape drive exposed the folly of this limit. Instead of attending an important conference, I converted the resource manager to use a full-byte counter for tape drives.)

The current version of the support uses byte counters, is flexible and general because resources can easily be added, and takes two, rather than one, 32-bit words per job. The increased storage cost (1000 words, 4000 bytes!?) is minimal compared to the major benefits of the cleaner design.

Another time, I was a little smarter. For each job on the HASP 4.0 system, two table entries were maintained: a job queue entry and a job information entry. The nth job queue entry and the nth job information entry belonged to the same job, so a common performance modification took advantage of the size of these elements being even multiples of two, and replaced a multiply instruction with a shift instruction. A co-worker suggested this modification, but I resisted, as our machine had the high-speed multiply feature installed and the "performance" modification would only have reduced the code's generality.

Watch out for excessively clever solutions. Be alert to the current cost of what you are saving. The industry is changing constantly, and last year's efficient practice may be terrible today. Saving a little storage, CPU time, or disk space is seldom worth the risk of having to rework the modification. Instead, anticipate expansion of function and leave some room for it.

Fast Assembler Language Coding

Sometimes, despite what I have recommended, you will have to squeeze a routine for speed. Have the facts at hand before you start.

On the XDS Sigma 7, register-to-register operations (implemented by referencing the first 16 memory locations) are *slower* than storage references, a shock if you are used to the IBM System/370 register-to-register operations, which are that machine's quickest instructions.

In the DEC PDP-11, the program counter is the PC register, one of the eight general registers. On some systems, a load of the PC register is faster than a branch instruction. On the DEC VAX-11/780, such usage plays havoc with the pre-fetching unit, even though the VAX is considered program-compatible with the PDP-11.

On an IBM System/360, when unaligned operands (fullword operands not aligned on a full word, or halfword operands not aligned on a half word) are encountered, a program check occurs. On the IBM System/370, execution proceeds, but at a considerably slower pace.

On smaller System/370 models, the code segment:

```
L    R1,6(R6)
LA   R1,0(,R1)
LTR  R1,R1
```

is *faster* than the equivalent:

```
ICM  R1,7,7(R6)
```

75

The preceding four examples are by no means complete, or intended as a guide to danger spots in machine timing. Such a work would be much larger. They should show you that instruction speeds are not always consistent or sensible. Before you write the fastest ten lines of code known to mankind, check the instruction timing charts to be sure the new routine isn't actually slower than the code you are replacing. Common sense here is no match for the facts.

Tight Use of Memory

Older systems often forced us to work very hard to conserve memory. Today, tight use of memory may represent normal or pathological programming decisions.

Brooks† discusses the normal case very well. He explains that we may exchange memory for computer time and input/output operations over a wide range to achieve system performance goals.

Unfortunately, some programmers, used to the constraints of very small systems, are fanatical about saving storage. Consider the half-byte arithmetic I discussed under "Balanced Efficiency." Single insert and store character instructions replace two sequences of five instructions that perform the half-byte insert and store. The instruction sequence overhead was 52 bytes, or 13 words. The half-byte arithmetic did offer a fair savings in storage, but only because the table it accessed was large. Similar tight storage coding would probably be inappropriate were the table a tenth its actual size: 100 instead of 1000 entries. Were the table a hundredth its actual size (10 entries), the "tight" code would actually waste both computer time *and* storage.

Before setting out to save storage, do some simple arithmetic to be sure you are not overreacting. For small tables, code for clarity, not storage economy. Remember that clever coding takes extra time to design, code, debug and, most of all, pass

---

†Frederick Brooks, Jr., *The Mythical Man-Month* (Reading, Mass.: Addison-Wesley, 1975), Chapter 9.

to a new individual. Leverage is the key — save your best storage saving tricks for the biggest effect. If you think you can save
a byte in a table with ten entries, usually the difficulty of the
change will greatly outweight the benefit. When the table becomes 100 entries, the difficulty probably still dwarfs the benefit.
At 1000 entries, the one-byte savings begins to look promising.

Use Higher Level Languages

A computing folk tale begins, "programs written in assembler language are more efficient than programs written in a higher level language." The folk tale has been wrong for quite a while. Optimizing compilers, able to locate innermost loops and move extraneous code outside the loop, may take more care with the compiled program than the programmer would with the same routine written in assembler. A change in programming languages does not instill a programmer with efficient coding practices.

The truth today is that an assembler language routine has more latitude in efficiency than the equivalent routine written in a higher level language. With careful work, assembler can be more efficient; with haste and lack of care, it will be less efficient. Certainly, assembler language coding is slower to produce, harder to debug, and harder to turn over to another programmer. Remember that a better algorithm will offer more dramatic performance benefits than better implementation of the same algorithm.

Some friends of mine, heady with pride in their skill, wrote an entire accounting system in assembler, including the report-writing facilities. They have had a hard time escaping from their product, and the monthly requests for changes in the monthly reports mean long hours for them. "Next time," they vow, "ANSI COBOL."

Another group of friends wrote a statistical analysis program for the IBM 7094 in assembler language. As the sun set on the 7094, they planned a new version. For the 360, they rewrote the program using ANSI FORTRAN IV in so rigid a manner that they didn't use features peculiar to IBM FORTRAN IV. *Result:* they can install the new version on Univac, CDC, or almost any large system, with very little work. Their user community (and thus financial base) is significantly larger than in the 7094 days. Perhaps their software is less efficient, but certainly the program is beneficial to many more users, because it affords a greater good for a greater number.

The decision to program a routine, module, or, worse yet, a system in assembler language should be reviewed thoroughly and regarded as a desperate measure. Assembler language programs cost substantially more for the same function than any other programming language. Any line of reasoning that requires assembler must be suspect.

Portability

Be cautioned that simply using a compiler language provides no guarantee of machine independence. Use of octal or hexadecimal input and output can tie you to a particular machine, and word-oriented logical AND and OR functions (rather than string-oriented) make you dependent on the system's word size. Worse yet, some compilers support in-line assembler language code or allow reference to specific machine registers.

Some hardware dependencies are more subtle. On a cartographic program conversion project, we used integer arithmetic for all processing because the system lacked floating-point hardware and the overhead of simulation would have slowed the system too much. Although integer arithmetic supported our data representation, we encountered a bug in calculating distances between points:

$$X^2 + Y^2 = Z^2$$

the famous Pythagorean relationship, produced intermediate products too large for the fixed-point word size. We computed this value using the simulated floating-point support. Changes in machine word size can produce subtle difficulties.

Language interpretation problems can limit portability. On the same cartographic project, we discovered that the FORTRAN compiler for our new system interpreted the precedence of logical operations in the reverse order from the old:

$$(A.AND.B.OR.C.AND.D)$$

instead of receiving the standard interpretation:

$$((A.AND.B).OR.(C.AND.D))$$

was compiled as:

$$(A.AND.(B.OR.C).AND.D)$$

This bug took a little while to isolate. I agree with the many authors who recommend additional parentheses for clarity in mathematical expressions. If, instead of memorizing the rules, we write for people, the code becomes more portable, no matter what.

However, machine-dependent compiler languages are not necessarily bad. Users of languages such as PL360† and IBM's PL/S‡ report the improved programmer productivity normally associated with a compiler language without the higher storage costs compiler languages like PL/I, COBOL, and FORTRAN exact. Your application may not require portability.

You must address portability as a design decision as important as the programming language you choose. Programs do not become portable by accident or default. Coding standards are necessary to achieve machine independence. Sometimes portability demands that you deny yourself some features of the programming language.

---

†Niklaus Wirth, "PL360, A Programming Language for the 360 Computer," Journal of the ACM, 15 (1968).

‡See *Guide to PL/S II*, IBM, form C28-6794. Unfortunately no PL/S compiler is generally available outside the IBM Corporation.

"Efficient" Coding in Higher Level Languages

Higher level languages offer several important benefits for system implementation: the ability of a new programmer to take over another's work comes to mind. Unfortunately some "efficient" coding practices have evolved that counter our goal of clarity in system code. The two described here, in FORTRAN, are typical examples to be avoided.

One popular second-generation FORTRAN compiler called the exponentiation routine whenever it saw $X**2$, rather than compiling $X*X$. As a consequence many programmers go out of their way to code $X*X$ when they mean X^2. This kind of "efficient" coding should be avoided for two reasons. First, the resultant coding may not reflect program or programmer intent. Second, most third-generation compilers are smart enough to compile $X**2$ as $X*X$, and $X**3$ as $X*X*X$, so that the formerly efficient practice becomes useless trivia. Remember that such coding practices are tedious and labor intensive, and our objective is to reduce the time we take to write working programs.

A multidimensional array can be handled by the compiler, or coded as a singly dimensioned array, with the programmer computing the subscripts. Some programmers delight in showing their prowess by using the latter technique. Discourage this pathological practice. Compiler writers work very hard on efficient code for array processing, and usually the compiler is better at it than you are. If you and the compiler are only equal, the compiler should get the nod, since writing unnecessary indexing code will only slow your project down. (The second-generation IBM 7040's FORTRAN compiler, for example, generates the variable-length multiply and accumulate (VMA) instruction when handling arrays, and the resultant code is faster than the FORTRAN programmer can write.)

The sound reasons for using compiler languages should not be abandoned simply to chase a couple of machine cycles. Remember that we chose compiler languages to escape just this sort of trivia.

Processor Recovery

Techniques now exist which allow programs to recover from software failures. I call this ability "processor recovery." I used to pay little attention to recovery. I believed that if I debugged my work carefully, failures would never occur. This may be true, but I no longer think that way. When a system supports upwards of a hundred on-line users, the legitimate pressure to remain available despite a few lines of bad code is extremely high.

MVS did not bring with it the system functions needed to implement processor recovery: I developed my best recoverable processor for OS/MFT. The newer support (ESTAE, SDUMP) does provide more information than the older support (STAE, SNAP).

A recovery routine should be designed to:

1. Preserve whatever information is necessary to resolve the problem.
2. Clear out the failing transaction in as few instructions as possible (making the recovery routine a small target for potential overlays).
3. Return to the failed code.

The recoverable processor I wrote validates job passwords. In clearing the failing transaction, I assumed that our code, not the transaction, was bad, and allowed the job to run if the code failed. Otherwise, a condition might have occurred due to soft-

ware problems where I could not run anything, even to correct
the problem!

This support allows 100 percent availability with less than
100 percent reliable software. Processor recovery does not replace reliable programs, it provides a bridge to them.

Don't Skimp on Operator Commands

You may wish you hadn't! In designing a software package, resist the temptation to try to shorten the schedule by reducing or eliminating the query and modification support you offer the operator. If the package does not work well under stress, the operator commands will allow you to determine what is wrong, and possibly adjust things manually, while you prepare a correction. If the package works but has performance problems, good operator commands can be a big help in isolating the difficulty. If the package is a complete success, the operators will make good use of powerful, easy-to-use displays and controls.

Operator commands are always easier to prepare as part of the development process than to retrofit later. When they are part of development, they can be used to help debug the package. As afterthoughts, they become high-visibility hassles.

User Documentation

When time-sharing first appeared, users voiced three major complaints:

1. The system was often unavailable.
2. It processed work very slowly.
3. The documentation didn't match the software.

Since then, the first two complaints have been attacked aggressively. In that time, equipment and techniques have appeared that will allow us to solve the third problem as well.

Both on the hardware and software front, availability and reliability have shown dramatic improvements. The techniques described in this book should improve your software reliability. We are finally approaching the dream of the 1960s: a "computer utility" on a par with other public utilities. Today's high-performance systems reduce, and nearly eliminate, the need to optimize the program, programmer, and user for the computer.

Documentation has lagged behind, but methods and equipment are coming to the rescue here as well. Since the days when college students worked 60 to 80 hours a week on their systems, time-sharing software has grown faster than timely documentation could be delivered to the systems' users. I believe that only on-line documentation distributes information in a timely enough fashion. Fortunately, both the cost of on-line storage and terminal data rates have improved sufficiently to provide an alternative. To offer maximum usability, we cannot settle simply for printed documentation stored on-line. Better techniques are possible and desirable.

IBM's TSO system† includes a HELP command that retrieves information about each system command. Options allow the user to select as little or as much information as is needed. Typically, a user may request information about a specific keyword of a command. One possible extension to this facility would include command groupings by function. Since some commands bridge two or more classes of functions, provision for this would need to be made. (The SUBMIT command is both a batch command, because it submits a job for background, and a dataset command, because it reads a dataset to build the job.) The inexperienced user would no longer have to deduce that because ALLOCATE creates a dataset, DELETE removes it, rather than ERASE, PURGE, REMOVE, or SCRATCH. Today, a typical HELP dataset may contain around two million characters of information, not a high price to pay for immediate availability of documentation.

But we can go a step further. IBM's Structured Programming Facility (SPF)‡ supports a HELP key whose operation complements what the user is already doing: under each system function, specific hints and information are displayed. When pressed after an error message, the help key prompts SPF to give more information about the error.

Time-sharing systems were originally developed for terminals that type at 10 to 15 characters per second. The faster devices allow us to be a little more liberal in the information we display. A printed page with 60 lines of information can be typed on a 120-character-per-second terminal in about 40 seconds. If that much information is needed, it should be available.

Don't be satisfied with a project plan that simply includes a "user's guide" as the system's documentation. Consider the cost and benefit of on-line documentation. Chances are, you can provide the terminal user with good information without reference to a separate book.

---

†*OS/VS2 TSO Command Language Reference*, IBM, form C28-0646, describes the system. Unfortunately, the document doesn't show the full power of the HELP facility.

‡*Time Sharing Option 3270 Display Support and Structured Programming Facility*, IBM, form H20-1975.

What's Wrong With Flowcharts

When I first studied programming, flowcharting was in flower. Flowcharts aren't bad, but superior techniques have appeared.

Under "Structured Programming," I didn't give you the complete story: theoretical work shows that any program can be written using only three constructs. These constructs are: IF . . . THEN . . . ELSE (decision making), DO . . . WHILE (looping), and sequential instructions. Further, practical experience has shown that programs constructed strictly from these building blocks are much easier to design, code, implement, and maintain. The control flow of a structured program is much easier to follow than flow in an unstructured program, so that the flowchart becomes less important. One can as easily read the program itself as the flowchart to determine how it works.

At a seminar I attended, the leader asked if any of us used flowcharts heavily, and one chap indicated he did and explained why. "Our customer demands them as part of the deliverable. We use an automatic program to generate them from our code." When asked about flowchart quality, he explained that it depended on the quality of the program comments and the overall program structure. The automatic program eliminates the need for flowchart updating, a costly, often neglected part of maintenance. Certainly, outdated flowcharts are useless debugging tools.

While flowcharts are often touted as a design tool, the popularity of automatic flowchart generators suggests that some programmers aren't coding from flowcharts, or at least not from the final version.

Flowcharts are oriented towards the computer programmer. Members of the general population, and especially the management population, don't necessarily understand them. Thus, they can be a tool to confuse and obscure the facts. Even in the best hands, flowcharts emphasize program control flow, rather than program logic. The flowchart is a map of where the program is going, rather than what decisions it makes. Admittedly, many of us have learned to deduce the latter from the former, but that's backwards.

Even for programmers, flowcharts aren't necessarily easy to read. The instructor for my CDP† review course recommended that if we encountered a flowchart in the examination, we should choose an answer at random and forge ahead. He argued that in a 50-minute, 60-question examination one didn't have time to interpret a flowchart well enough to get the question right. Our attempts to answer his sample flowchart questions demonstrated both that the time involved was excessive, and that flowcharts are very difficult to read. (After long study, many of us got the questions wrong!)

The parallel between flowcharts and illuminated manuscripts is too tempting to pass up. Both products require special artistic talents and equipment to prepare, and take extraordinary amounts of time to do properly. They are both extremely "manual" products.

Fortunately, we may use an alternative technique. Decision tables allow us to achieve many of the goals we look for in flowcharts, and offer some additional benefits.

---

† Certificate in Data Processing, administered by the Institute for Certification of Computer Professionals, 304 East 45th Street, New York, NY 10017.

Decision Tables

Often we must handle a large number of binary conditions. A technique of charting them, decision tables,† breaks out all the possible conditions, all the possible actions, and meshes the two. Accidentally forgotten conditions are eliminated. Decision tables connect input and output far more effectively than flowcharts.

We had a modification where three different actions might be taken depending on terminal type, line type, and user input. We found the following decision table focused the requirements rapidly and painlessly.

We constructed the decision table by listing on a sheet of paper, one to a line, the conditions we were to test: terminal type, whether the RJE line had transparency feature, and finally whether the T field for the terminal was set to TN. Following these conditions, we listed the actions we might take: PN translation, which eliminates characters not in the 60-character PN font, BSC translation, which eliminates data link control characters, or no translation. To the right, vertically, we indicated the combinations of conditions that might occur, and below them the actions that we would take. The table we wrote follows.

What's nice about this decision table? *First, we can easily read the table.* For example, if we are using a multi-leaving terminal (C1 is M), the line is transparent (C2 is Y), and T = TN (C3 is Y) then rule R4 is used, and we perform no translation

---

† I recommend Raymond Fergus, "Decision Tables — What, Why, and How," in Daniel Couger and Robert Knapp, eds., *Systems Analysis Techniques* (New York: Wiley, 1974), pp. 162–179, as a tutorial for decision table preparation.

RJE Upper/Lower Case Support Decision Table							
		Rules					
		R1	R2	R3	R4	R5	R6
Condition Statements		Condition Entries					
C1	Terminal Type (H) Hardware (M) Multi-Leaving	H	H	M	M	M	M
C2	Transparent Line	-	-	Y	Y	N	N
C3	T=TN	N	Y	N	Y	N	Y
Action Statements		Action Entries					
A1	PN Translate	X		X		X	
A2	BSC Translate (minimal)		X				X
A3	No Translate				X		

(take action A3). Decision tables can serve as good communication devices between programmer and user. Redraw this decision table as a flowchart and compare readability. Decision tables allow us to depict complex relationships without a complicated structure.

Second, no special tools or skills are needed to prepare it. Unlike a flowchart, drawn with a template, quadrule paper, and a drafting pen to produce neat results, only a ruler and pen or typewriter are needed to make a decision table.

Third, we can determine if the decision table covers all possible conditions. For any decision table, no more rules are possible than total number of possible conditions. Similarly, and more importantly, a decision table is complete if all possible rules are covered.

For this decision table, each condition may take on two possible values, so that the total number of possible conditions is 2*2*2, or 8. (C1 may be H or M; C2 and C3 may each be Y or N.) Therefore, eight rules are possible. We only show six rules because condition C2, transparency, is ignored if C1 is H. (The — entered under rules R1 and R2 indicates we don't care about condition C2.) Rules R1 and R2 could each be expanded to two rules, one with C2 showing Y and one with C2 showing N. This would give us all eight rules, so our decision table is complete. We eliminated the two redundant rules for simplicity, since the action taken in rules R1 and R2 does not depend on C2.

Decision tables allow us to describe and study program logic in a simpler and more compact way than flowcharts. Further, we can quickly test a decision table to determine if all logical conditions have been covered, a difficult process with a flowchart. For more about the use of decision tables, particularly in testing, see the "Test Every Branch" chapter.

Error Messages

Considerable follow-up trouble can be purchased with short-sighted error messages. Error messages should describe the error condition lucidly enough to permit the user to react appropriately without further assistance.

Years ago, flooding the user with an octal dump was considered good form when handling errors. With the shift to third-generation hardware, a new technique appeared: the user was flooded with even more pages of *hexadecimal* dump. Actually the third-generation hardware offers much more memory, so that we have plenty of room for automatic error diagnosis coding.

I once developed a modification that returned two four-digit numbers when there was a problem. After the first dozen calls, asking me what the numbers meant, I rewrote the modification to invoke a formatting routine. *Result:* no more calls!

One system utility announces CONFLICTING DCB PARAMETERS when it cannot process a dataset. Unfortunately this message reflects three different conditions: invalid description of the input file, invalid description of the output file, or a conflict between the input and output file definitions. Think how much more helpful the three messages:

CONFLICTING DCB PARAMETERS FOR SYSUT1

CONFLICTING DCB PARAMETERS FOR SYSUT2

CONFLICTING DCB PARAMETERS BETWEEN SYSUT1 AND SYSUT2

would be. But we could still do more with this error message. Since the program detected a conflict, it ought to tell us what the conflict is. If it found, for example, that block size was not an even multiple of logical record length on a fixed-block file, it should tell us just that, preferably in clear text, rather than with a message number.

Stretched to the extreme, poor error messages give us the classic computer game: the machine says, "enter input," the human does so, and the machine responds, "invalid input, re-enter." Since the machine has more patience than the human, it usually wins. Messages should do more than merely indicate the presence of an error, they should tell where the error is, what the program is going to do, and what the user should do about it. Programs that echo bad input with a sentinel line below, indicating where in the line an error was detected, can get by with far fewer messages; knowing the location of the syntax error helps the user correct it. For example,

```
DISPLAY INPUT=DISK,OUTPUT=SYSPRINT,FORMAT=BOTH
                                              *
ERR001 INVALID OPTION FOR KEYWORD
```

Note that the sentinel line, marking the error, eliminates the need for text substitution in the error message.

Since I mentioned keywords, let me tell another war story. One program remembers the current keyword, and reflects this when an error is reported. Unfortunately it doesn't update the keyword for the message soon enough; rewriting the preceding example:

```
DISPLAY INPUT=DISK,OUTPUT=SYSPRINT,FORMAT=BOTH
ERR001 INVALID OPTION IN THE OUTPUT KEYWORD
```

Only the experienced hand will remember that the keyword in error is actually the one *after* the keyword mentioned in the message. (Just as in the previous example, the program expects ALL instead of BOTH for the FORMAT= option.)

When using OS/VS JCL, the error message DATASET NOT FOUND actually means dataset not *cataloged*. The system issues the 213 ABEND code when it cannot *find* a dataset. With practice, one may learn such mysteries, but if we set out to describe error conditions clearly, we can save the user a lot of confusion.

Once the error has been detected and the user informed, what should we do next? Practices vary, but putting yourself in the position of the user will help you decide. The worst possible approach is to abort the run at the first sign of trouble, flushing the input stream. (I am reminded of one early second-generation FORTRAN compiler. If errors were detected, messages were issued and the compiler *stopped*. Further phases of the compiler were not entered. The user would correct all the compiler-detected errors and resubmit, expecting execution this time. Unfortunately later phases of the compiler, ones not entered because the compiler abandoned the previous compilation, would discover further errors and stop compilation again. Since turnaround on the system took many hours, novices could grow old fighting their way through the phases of the compiler.) Your users would much prefer a processor that kept plugging along, possibly issuing extraneous error messages, but checking all the input thoroughly. It shouldn't take ten runs to detect ten syntax errors.

I recommend human engineering: make your software easy for people to use. Unlike systems programmers, users of COBOL and FORTRAN, for example, are not prepared to resolve their problems by reviewing mountains of hexadecimal numbers. The user's experience must be taken into consideration. An error message review, in which each error message is presented to end users, along with system action taken, can eliminate many incorrect assumptions made by the programmers. One of the few concrete ways users can evaluate systems programming work is through error messages. The messages are the most visible part of your product.

Abend

Don't. Most operating systems include a facility whereby an easily coded instruction, macro, or system call will produce a brief diagnostic (PROGRAM ABENDED, CODE-U0020) and leave the user awash in a hexadecimal or octal dump. Although this practice may be helpful to the programmer during development, abends sprinkled throughout the program tarnish the finished product.

With ABEND termination, too much data and too little information are left to the user. OS/360's usability improved dramatically when system error messages were implemented to supplement the system's abend codes. Instead of just saying ABEND 213, the system now reports the name of the dataset it couldn't find. Users wishing that information no longer have to examine the contents of register 4 and then burrow into the dump to extract the dataset name; the system now does that chore for them.

Follow the general techniques suggested in the "Error Messages" chapter and develop messages to report problems. If 64 (hex) bytes off register 4 are significant to the problem, as with the system 213 abend, extract that information and put it in the message. If the contents of register 15 indicate an error return, report both the value and a one-line description of the error condition.

Our design goal for errors must be to eliminate the need of a user examining dump data to determine the cause of problems. The time spent interpreting a dump to uncover predictable error conditions represents a dead loss to the end user. Further, the effort to read the dump distracts the user from resolving the original error condition.

Response Messages

The same consideration for the end user applies to normal response messages as for error messages.† The issue is not the terseness or verbosity of the messages but the data they contain specific to the user request.

Compare:

```
output nohold dest(rmt03)
JOB ROUTED
READY
```

with

```
output nohold dest(rmt03)
SYS033A(JOB00345) ROUTED TO RMT3
READY
```

The message in the second example conveys much more information than that in the first. If the system is performing a conversion from user input format to internal format, echoing messages with the internal data converted back to user format provide the user with a considerable degree of comfort that the system understood and acted correctly on his request. Note that

---

† For a more complete treatment of this, see Ben Shneiderman, *Software Psychology* (Cambridge, Mass.: Winthrop Publishers, 1980), particularly Chapters 9 through 12.

simply echoing the input text provides less assurance than the double conversion. In the example, the destination (RMT3) was converted to internal format and back for printing, and the job selected by the system for routing was reported back to the user.

However, the first format is not all bad; some system response is better than none. Early OS/360 operators liked the HASP spooling system partly because HASP operator commands always elicited some responses from the computer: "OK" became the computer equivalent of "uhuh." Since many of the OS commands didn't then offer confirmation messages, the operator often had a feeling that the system wasn't listening.

Well-designed response messages will give the system user a feeling of comfort that his wishes are being acted on. You can accomplish this without flooding the user with messages.

Humane Input

A nightmare system would join inhumane input formats and baffling error messages. Thought, study, and experience are required to develop input formats that are easy and natural to use.† Here are a few case studies.

The registration form for a major computer conference once required a one-letter code indicating position in the organization. At least one "speaker" (the most common position) is present at every session in the conference. Speakers were expected to enter A for their position code. The secretary of the organization uses the code S as do dozens of speakers who don't read the instructions carefully enough.

As another example, sometimes system operation defies the principle every kindergarten teacher knows: "if they might hurt themselves, give them scissors with rounded points!" A major time-sharing system is distributed with a D command, which deletes datasets. Since the D key is very near the E key on a terminal, a single incorrect keystroke will destroy rather than edit a dataset. Further, under the editor D means delete data lines, a painful surprise to the user who, familiar with other editors, meant DOWN, intending to move deeper into the dataset.

Along this same line, an earlier terminal system's INPUT command allowed data entry into both new and existing data files. When referencing an existing data file, INPUT defaulted

---

† For a more thorough treatment of this, see Tom Gilb and Gerald Weinberg, *Humanized Input* (Cambridge, Mass.: Winthrop Publishers, 1977).

to clearing the file instead of appending. Many users lost data by forgetting the APPEND option, which should have been the default.

As a general rule, include protection against automatic data destruction in your software. Techniques similar to that used on most tape recorders, where two keys must be depressed to record a tape, are appropriate. Queries of the form: "Are you sure I should destroy this file?" should be included.

When we first installed private procedure library support, the control card looked like this:

$$/*\text{PROCLIB DSN=dsname}[/\text{password}]$$

After some user feedback, however, we expanded the syntax to:

$$/*\text{PROCLIB} \begin{Bmatrix} \text{DSN=} \\ \text{DSNAME=} \end{Bmatrix} \text{dsname}[/\text{password}] \begin{Bmatrix} \\ ,\text{any text} \end{Bmatrix}$$

The DSN= keyword suggested that the new control card was similar to a job control language (JCL) DD statement. Some users wanted to code DSNAME= or follow the dataset name with ,DISP=SHR. Different sorts of users have different perceptions of the system; in writing a JES2 modification it didn't occur to me that the new control card would be perceived as similar to the JCL DD statement, but some of our users did see it in that light.

You might expect me to advocate processors that accept English-language input, but I do not. Experience shows me that simply claiming the input format is English doesn't make it any easier for the users. Does anyone believe, for example, that the COBOL programming language can be mastered simply by doing well in high school business English? Certainly choosing key-words that match English makes the spelling easier, but more work is necessary for clean input formats.

Our mother tongue is far too ambiguous for direct use in today's data processing systems. Recently we installed a new interactive editor, and I had enormous trouble moving deeper into the file I was editing. A more knowledgeable friend took me aside and explained that even though all the editors I had ever used took UP to mean move towards the start of the file, and DOWN to mean move towards the end of the file, the new editor assumed the display was stationary, and the dataset moved. Therefore, UP, that is, moving the scrolled dataset upwards, moves the current line pointer towards the end of the dataset. My friend could not explain, however, why TOP still meant the start of the dataset so that one now moves DOWN to the TOP. To prevent confusion, English-language controls need careful thought before implementation.

Modulo problems can also baffle the user. If a common routine is used to convert numeric input to binary and the stored format of the input has a narrower range than the common routine supports, check the converted number before storing. For example, when processing:

```
//jobname JOB ...,PRTY=nn,...
```

if nn is stored in a half-byte, check for a value above 15 before storing, so that the user won't wonder why

```
//jobname JOB ...,PRTY=20,...
```

gave priority 4. Instead, warn that the value exceeds system limits.

Humane input formats may appear to be optional improvements. Actually, programs tolerant of user tendencies take the desired action more often. Programs that take correct actions prevent unproductive disputes between the programmer ("It did what you told it!") and the user ("Who designed this format?"). When your users report difficulties with input formats, consider whether the requirements can be made more natural. Better still, log user input errors automatically to broaden the sample and reduce the friction inherent in error reporting. The users' errors form a good basis for improving the system. A good project plan will include time to respond to common errors after early user testing.

Automatic Spelling Correction

Generally, computer systems have shown no tolerance for misspelled keywords. Following the accepted technique, the programmer prepares a list of valid keywords and compares the user input until a match is detected or the list ends. Automatic detection and correction of mistyped keywords† can be implemented with relative ease, and should be considered for new systems.

Psychological research has indicated that around 80 percent of all misspelled words differ by one of four ways from the correct spelling:‡

1. One character is incorrect,
2. An extra character has been inserted,
3. One character was omitted, or
4. Two adjacent characters are transposed.

A few cautions are recommended. If automatic spelling correction is attempted for abbreviations of keywords, the chance of improper correction increases, because the shorter fields are less redundant. Generally, keywords must be different

---

†I am indebted to Gary D. Schultz, now with Northwest Industries, for describing his experiences with this support.

‡ From Howard L. Morgan, "Spelling Correction in Systems Programs," *Communications of the ACM* 13, no. 2 (February 1970), pp. 90–94. The reference includes a detailed discussion of automatic spelling correction, a good bibliography, and a cunning comparison routine written in System/360 assembler language.

enough to prevent miscorrection. If two proposed keywords are so close that they match under one of the four tests, they are too similar to be safe. Special precautions should be taken with keywords that have permanent effects. It shouldn't be possible to delete a file when a misspelled keyword is automatically corrected. Inform the invoked processor that the keyword was misspelled and corrected rather than detected normally, so that it can decide whether to trust the correction.

How effective is this support? One operating version scans keywords for a tape library system, and users, generally experienced programmers, like the facility but aren't wild about it. I suspect that, among nonprogrammers, it would be much more popular. Other systems, driving video terminals, recall the invalid command to the screen, allowing user correction and reentry.

Make some provision for user error recovery when designing a program. If you can do more than simply say what's wrong, do so. Your users will appreciate your thoughtfulness.

Top Down Implementation

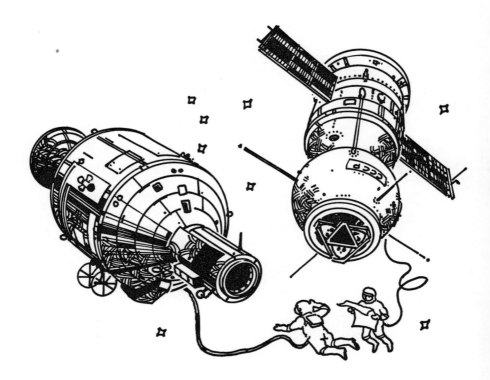

As I understand it, top down implementation of a system means coding and testing the interfaces *first*. Thus, the most difficult part of a large system, communication, becomes the most important task and receives the most attention.

My experience with top down implementation is more "in the breach than the observance," following instead the time-honored system implementation technique: after the system is designed down to the level of individual modules, the modules are coded and tested in isolation, using specially developed driver modules. The modules' interfacing logics are tested and debugged, but only with drivers, not with the real system. At intervals the individual modules are collected and merged, and system testing begins. (Imagine the Apollo and Soyuz spacecraft, meeting 500 miles above the Earth, and the astronauts coming out, the Russians to examine the round US docking sleeve, and the Americans to study the triangular USSR docking sleeve.)

These stressful exercises are often called *system builds*. Using this technique, the interfaces need a lot of debugging late in the implementation process, the busiest time.

Even jigsaw puzzle manufacturers use a different approach. They make a whole puzzle, and then cut it up. Thus, they are sure it will fit back together. Is there another way we can go about system implementation? Top down implementation, programming the interfaces first, can allow us to reverse the emphasis. Instead of first giving attention to the processing components of the system, we can first develop the interfaces. Dummy drivers now replace processing components.

My experience shows that interface problems tend to be the nastiest sort, the hardest to resolve. They take on many forms. For example, if the same mapping macro is not used on both sides of the interface, data fields may not mesh. (DS 0H and DS XL2 both generate a two-byte data field, but only the DS 0H aligns the field on a halfword. As a result, this discrepancy will "work" half the time, only to fail later, when an "irrelevant" change is made. Top down implemention allows us more opportunities for this failure to occur earlier.) Also, the interface control block may be built in a memory area inappropriate for the recipient (it may be deleted prior to recipient use, or be inaccessible to the recipient), or the interface may have hidden bugs not obvious under the light load of dummy test cases. If we wait until system build, as described, to discover these flaws, we are forced to debug our interfaces twice: once for the test drivers and once for the real system. Why not just do the work once and get the major problems out of the way early?

How can we break our old habits? During project planning, remind the team that interfaces are the hardest part of the job. (Your experiences undoubtedly show this.) Then advance a plan that focuses early attention on the interfaces. Remember that once implementation has begun, plans are hard to change.

What About Dataset Security?

When building new system services, we must always be sensitive to existing security mechanisms, lest we build an unlocked back door into the system.

I had finished testing my first attempt at dynamic procedure library allocation (see "Humane Input") and was describing my brilliance to a friend. He listened attentively, and, when I finished acquainting him with the mysteries of dynamic allocation and error message generation, he asked, bless him, "What about password protected datasets?" I thought a moment and realized that they were no problem at all: the dynamic proclib support could read anyone's dataset, regardless of protection, because JES2 enjoyed this privilege. I concluded that I had to allow password checking for JES2 to close the security exposure.

When a system task performs functions for a user, special cautions must be observed to ensure that normal system checking mechanisms are not circumvented.

Sunset Support

System malfunctions often occur due to combinations of events not predicted when designing the system. "Sunset" coding, support required only when something ends, can often be overlooked, particularly when designing an operating system data file.

Password protection for datasets, as implemented under OS/360, comes to mind as a package weak in sunset support. Access to a password-protected dataset is permitted under OS only if the operator supplies the correct password. Special system checking occurs during dataset allocation and deletion. All passwords known to the system are stored in a single dataset together with the names of the datasets they refer to.

When a password-protected dataset is deleted, the entry in the password dataset is not automatically removed. It must be manually deleted to prevent the password dataset from growing without bound!

Why did this problem occur? I'm not sure, but here's what I think. When the TSO terminal system was added as a feature of OS, dataset password protection changed from a feature normally used only for operating system datasets to a function users often invoke. Consequently the use made of the facility changed both in number of datasets protected and the kinds of datasets protected. While you might reasonably expect a systems programmer to understand and compensate for the lack of automatic password deletion on dataset deletion, such expectations are unreasonable for terminal users. They don't understand the system's internal operation and couldn't care less.

We can draw two lessons from this: system actions surrounding the end of things (a job, a dataset, or a record in a system dataset) demand special attention to prevent incomplete termination and second, a dramatic change in the user community associated with a system function may require reexamination of that function. The design may have assumed characteristics of the users or their usage that no longer apply. IBM now offers an optional dataset security system oriented toward terminal users: RACF.†

---

† See *IBM OS/VS2 MVS Resource Access Control Facility — General Information Manual*, IBM, form C28-0722.

Modular Changes

Whenever we install a modification, we should design it with updates, both to the base software and to our change, in mind. Ideally our changes should be as well isolated as possible. If the change involves adding code to a specific spot in the module, we can save considerable trouble later on by implementing the modification as a call to a new routine, which performs the function required and returns to the original code.

MODULAR CHANGE ILLUSTRATION

VENDOR ROUTINE   USER ROUTINE

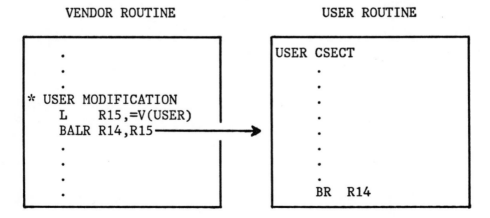

```
          .                         USER CSECT
          .                              .
          .                              .
* USER MODIFICATION                       .
    L    R15,=V(USER)                     .
    BALR R14,R15 ─────────────────▶       .
          .                              .
          .                              .
          .                              .
          .                         BR   R14
```

This technique adds an exit to the vendor code, centralizes our modification, and prepares us for rapid upgrading to new releases. We thus escape the system modification paradox:

111

changing the operating system to meet our needs and then discovering that our modifications delay our moving to new systems that would meet our needs better. We are also protected against having to adapt the modification to maintenance, whether new modules or just updates arrive. Unfortunately some modifications require a different approach. For example, if we expand information formerly stored in a halfword into a fullword, we may be forced to implement the changes as a few lines of code in many different places, instead of an exit, where many lines of code are installed in one place.

Simulation

Simulation has gained popularity as a systems analysis technique because of its wide applicability and low cost. We use it in operating systems modification to predict the effect of changes.

The Problem

Our system runs jobs, units of work that arrive randomly, are classified by the system (A, B, . . . E) based on size, and execute on the system for some length of time. The jobs execute in initiators, which have lists of classes of work they run. An initiator need not run all classes of work; a selection list of ACD, for example, is acceptable.

A proposal was advanced that the system examine the size of the queues and, based on workload, sort certain initiators' selection lists. I decided that simulation was an ideal way to study the proposed modification.

A friend agreed to write a program that extracted a list of the jobs run on a given day, including job class, read-in time, execution duration, and actual execution start time, all from our accounting information. Some simulation buffs might have preferred a randomly generated execution stream, but I wanted to avoid the analysis necessary to generate a good random stream, and liked the idea of speaking about the effect of a system modification on a specific day's workload.

113

My Technique

I toyed with learning the GPSS simulation language (probably the best approach), but instead wrote a large simulator program in FORTRAN IV. My friend's data file represented the system input; internal arrays formed the system queues and initiators, complete with adjustable settings.

Results

The simulator did not support hopes that the selection list shuffle algorithm would improve system throughput dramatically, so we didn't implement it. I learned several things: plotting real begin-execution time against simulated begin-execution time showed good correlation and suggested that the queueing theory model was accurate. Specific instrumentation for the simulated initiators showed that the first three classes in an initiator selection list account for practically all of the jobs the initiator runs (that is, a selection list of ACB is equivalent to a list of ACBDE). I found it very difficult to produce a "structured" program in FOR-TRAN. The simulator is a classic spaghetti string routine — a five-page main module and two half-page subroutines (paying lip service to modularity). However, unconditional GO TO's are eliminated. Finally, I learned once again that management always prefers to make decisions based on evidence rather than intuition. The simulator output reversed management sentiment about the initiator shuffler.

Simulation needn't be difficult or mysterious to be successful. Our relatively simple simulator provided a very accurate model of the operating system features we wanted to study, and allowed us to learn some things about our system.

Follow-up

1. Hold a "Structured Walkthrough" for a program you have written, or better still, one you are currently designing. If your design escapes modification, consider the walkthrough a failure and try again.

2. Find out which programming languages are in use at your installation and why. Then determine which programming languages would be most appropriate for your needs. Do they differ?

3. Take a program flowchart, preferably from a program you wrote, and write a "Decision Table" for it. Is the decision table easier to read? Does your decision table expose missing conditions?

SECTION 4

Coding Practices

My intent in this section is to describe coding techniques that reduce errors. The techniques can be used whenever assembler language code is written; they are independent of any particular program design.

You probably already use some of the practices I will recommend. In fact, I hope a few sound obvious and familiar to you. Others I suggest may seem arbitrary or unreasonable, but they work, often whether you believe in them or not. Unconditional branches, for example, may not seem intrinsically harmful, but they are. None of the following suggestions is theoretical. They all have reduced errors in professional programming environments.

Structured Programming

Rather than debate what is and what isn't structured, I will suggest structured techniques effective for assembler language coding: eliminate unconditional branches, don't branch backwards, and write one-page routines.

Many unconditional branches reflect bad programming and should be eliminated, particularly when paired with conditional branches:

```
BNE    loc1
B      loc2
```

This example, unless possibly at the very end of a routine, shrieks sloppy structure. Ideally all program branches should be conditional (BE, BL, BH, for example).

Don't branch backwards. Except when forming a loop, a conditional or unconditional branch backwards ("up" the listing page) reflects poor planning. Good code flows down the listing page, rather than hopping back and forth.

No subroutine should extend beyond a single listing page. If this discipline is followed, your system is built of small, easy-to-comprehend routines. Such small routines are easily read, and their function deduced. Suspend your worries about saving paper, and force the assembler to skip to a new page.

These simple disciplines will dramatically improve the code you write. You will make fewer mistakes, and the errors you make will be much easier to detect and correct.

Quirks of Assembler Language

Assembler language is a very powerful programming medium. That's bad because, compared to modern compilers, assemblers are far less able to make global examinations of the programs they process. For example, assemblers cannot detect misuse of variables. The language allows for code that assembles correctly but doesn't do what was desired:

Literal Specification

correct

```
        MVC   TARGET,=C'9'

        MVI   TARGET,C'9'

        . . .

TARGET DS   C
```

Both of these instructions move the character "9" into the field.

120

incorrect

```
            MVC  TARGET,C'9'
                 . . .
     TARGET DS   C
```

This last example is different. Although it resembles the first two, it moves the contents of location 249 (decimal representation of the character 9) into TARGET. That operation is probably not what was desired, but will most certainly assemble and execute.

Field Sizes

Halfwords and fullwords are different. Keep instructions, data, and literals in synchronization on this point:

correct

```
            LH   R1,=H'10'

            L    R1,=F'10'
```

Both of these instructions set register one to the value 10.

incorrect

```
            LH   R1,=F'10'

            L    R1,=H'10'
```

Both of these instructions assemble without error, but *neither* will set register one to the value 10.

370 Mask Instructions

The 370 "mask" instructions (CLM, STCM, and ICM) can also be trouble spots:

correct

```
                    STCM  R1,7,ADDR+1
                    . . .
         ADDR    DS    A
```

ADDR is a four-byte field with an address in the low-order three bytes. Here the computer loads the low-order three bytes of register 1 from the low-order three bytes of ADDR.

incorrect

```
                    STCM  R1,7,ADDR
                    . . .
         ADDR    DS    A
```

Here, the computer incorrectly loads the low-order three bytes of register 1 from the *high-order* three bytes of ADDR.

END Statement Syntax

We finish a program with the END statement.

correct

```
     END   ,                    CLOSE OUT THE PROGRAM
```

Comments on the END statement are tricky. Beware the operand field on the END statement.

incorrect

```
     END                        CLOSE OUT THE PROGRAM
```

Usually, CLOSE will be an undefined symbol. Trouble sets in when CLOSE is defined, and the link-editor thoughtfully uses that label as the start of your program, rather than the first program location.

Character Instruction Length Operand

This instruction moves the address of RTNE into BLKPTR:

correct

```
    MVC  BLKPTR-BLKDSECT(,R1),=A(RTNE)
```

incorrect

```
    MVC  BLKPTR-BLKDSECT(R1),=A(RTNE)
```

Here R1 will be interpreted as the length, not a base register, and therefore one byte will be moved into low storage!

LA Versus L

The choice between the load address (LA) instruction and the load (L) instruction can be confusing. Remember that LA adds up the base register, index register, and displacement, and puts that 24-bit quantity into a register. No memory reference is performed. L does the addition and then does a fetch from that location.

Literal Pool Positioning

Where you put your literals can affect program operation. The best approach is to tell the assembler where you want them:

correct

```
            AH   R1,=H'10'
            ...
            LTORG ,
            (literals generated here)
        A   DSECT
            ...
            END
```

incorrect

```
          AH    R1,=H'10'
          . . .
    A     DSECT
          . . .
          END
```

Guess where the literals go. That's right, at the end of DSECT A! Thus, since DSECTs do not generate data, even if this literal pool is addressable, it will not contain what you wanted. Usually the assembler will flag misplaced literals with addressability errors, but not always.

Typos of this sort cannot be eliminated. This list is not all-inclusive: I intend for it to alert you to the kinds of errors that are unique to assembler language. Reading the code, perhaps by someone other than the coder, is an effective, but not painless, way to cull the errors. Another technique is to develop standard coding practices that are safe from assembler quirks.

Smelling Dead Fish

Are there simple tests that detect error prone code? In an un-published study,† system modules with high error frequencies were examined to determine if similar coding techniques could be found. Two consistent predictors of trouble were found:

1. *TEMP Variables.* Any label containing the letters TEMP was a sure sign of problems. ATEMP, TEMP, TEMP1, or TEMP5A all reflected hasty, poor coding.

2. *Branch Mnemonics.* If the "positive" conditional branches (such as BE, BPL, BOV) and the "negative" branches (BNE, BNPL, BNOV) were counted, and the ratio between these computed, reliable programs had around 55–60 percent positive branches, while unreliable programs reflected 90–100 percent positive branches! We suspect that this again reflects hasty, sloppy coding, in that the programmer didn't take the time to consider what was ahead.

These simple tests can be used to rate modules being reviewed. Their simplicity makes the rating technique easy to apply and hard to question.

---

†My thanks to Gerald Weinberg for this information.

Use Memory Protect

When designing a program, try to use as many of the protective features of the operating system and hardware as you can. Perhaps the most important single example is memory protection.

In OS/360, system code usually runs with memory protection crippled. Thanks to improved design, the MVS practice is to cripple memory protection only when the program is actually going to change protected storage, and to restore protection immediately thereafter. Thus, if a register is accidentally cleared, a protection exception occurs rather than a low memory overlay.

Unfortunately some systems programmers still follow the OS/360 practice and write large blocks of code that run with protection crippled. When new code is written, a better practice is to minimize the time the program spends with memory protection crippled, since those times are very dangerous.

The first modification added to an operating system is often a generalized routine that renders all security provisions inoperative. On OS or VS systems, the vehicle is a Supervisor Call (SVC), frequently numbered 255. Try to avoid this change, since it offers many opportunities for problems and errors.

True-to-life example: a new customer began running a program at a service bureau, and each execution caused a system crash. The user's program was issuing SVC 255; control was returned with protect key zero and supervisor state. The program began blundering around, finally knocking out OS. The programmer had expected something much less powerful to result from SVC 255, as in its previous environment.

At minimum, a generalized routine that disables security should include a password check, at entry, to ensure that the caller knows what he or she is asking for. For example:

protected

```
SVC 255              OBTAIN KEY 0
DC  C'pswd'          CHECKED BY SVC 255
MVC 0(8,0),RESTPSW   SET NEW RESTART PSW
```

This SVC inspects the four-byte data field "pswd" immediately following the instruction that invokes it. If the password doesn't match expectations, the routine doesn't return with protection disabled.

Sample use of unprotected SVC 255 is as follows:

unprotected

```
SVC 255              OBTAIN KEY 0
MVC 0(8,0),RESTPSW   SET NEW RESTART PSW
```

This SVC 255 returns immediately in protect key zero, and the move characters instruction is allowed to occur. No check for a knowledgeable user is performed.

This change in protocol does not put a heavy strain on users but does eliminate the chance of accidental entry into supervisor state. For some thoughts on preventing intentional entry into supervisor state, see "System Integrity."

Reentrancy

Certain applications require that the programs used be reentrant, notably cases where multiple copies are in use. Reentrant code also offers performance benefits for the paging supervisor. For these reasons, on 370 systems, nonreentrant code is a nuisance.

Avoid problems by coding all assembler routines reentrantly. You can quickly learn the techniques:

1. Work areas must be separated from program data. (Under OS/VS, this data is often stored after the program save area, so that no additional base register is required.)
2. Instead of modifying program instructions dynamically, use the execute instruction and index registers. (For a discussion of "Dynamic Instruction Modification," see that chapter.)

Special precautions are necessary when using the IBM system macros in a reentrant environment. Many of the common functions (such as the OPEN macro) assemble in-line data areas that are subsequently modified by code generated by the macro. Other functions (such as WTO) build data areas you may wish to modify dynamically. Fortunately the IBM macros' LIST and EXECUTE forms support reentrant coding. Code the LIST form in a data area, copy the expanded text into allocated, modifiable storage, and, finally, code the EXECUTE form where you would have coded the normal macro usage before, pointing to the copied LIST form.

I have included a small reentrant program to clarify these points. The routine allocates storage using the GETMAIN macro, uses that storage as both a save area and a work area, uses LIST and EXECUTE forms of the system macros to maintain reentrancy, frees the storage when done, and returns. The execute instruction wasn't required for this example. I included it to demonstrate a reentrant instruction modification technique.

SAMPLE REENTRANT PROGRAM

```
RENT      CSECT
          ...                         (save registers)
          GETMAIN RU,LV=WORKSIZE      ALLOCATE WORK AREA
          ...                         (establish new save/work area)
          MVC    WTOTGT(WTOLEN),WTOLIST  COPY WTO LIST
          L      R1,CVTPTR            CVT BASE
          S      R1,=A(CVT-CVTRELNO)  BACKUP TO RELEASE NUMBER
          LA     R2,L'CVTRELNO        SET TEXT LENGTH
          EX     R2,COPYTXT           MOVE IN THE TEXT
          WTO    MF=(E,WTOTGT)        ISSUE WTO
          ...             (remove save/work area from chain)
          FREEMAIN RU,LV=WORKSIZE,A=(R1)  FREE WORK AREA
          ...                         (return)
WTOLIST   WTO    '..... IS THE RELEASE NUMBER',ROUTCDE=(11),MF=L
WTOLEN    EQU    *-WTOLIST
COPYTXT   MVC    WTOTGT+4(*-*),0(R1)  COPY TEXT
          LTORG
WORKAREA  DSECT
SAVEAREA  DS     18F                  SAVE AREA
WTOTGT    DS     (WTOLEN)X            WTO AREA
WORKSIZE  EQU    *-WORKAREA           LENGTH OF GETMAIN'D AREA
```

By always writing reentrant routines, you avoid the unpleasant chore of making your program reentrant later.

Dynamic Instruction Modification

Computer pioneers realized they had a major breakthrough when they developed methods whereby the computer could construct data and then execute it as a program. Although wholesale use of this ability by compilers and assemblers has profoundly shaped computing, retail use in assembler language programs should be avoided to prevent program readability problems.

clear

```
        LA    R2,LEN          GET DATA LENGTH
        SLR   R1,R1           CLEAR FOR
        IC    R1,OP             PROGRAM OPTION
        CH    R1,=H'2'        SIZE OK?
        BH    ERROR           NO, FAIL REQUEST
        MH    R1,=H'6'        ADJUST FUNCTION FOR MOVE LENGTH
        EX    R2,MOVE(R1)     DO THE MOVE
        ...
MOVE    MVC   ...
        MVZ   ...
        MVN   ...
```

Depending on input values (0, 1, or 2) the routine moves characters, zones only, or numerics only.

obscure

```
         IC    R1,OP
         STC   R1,TGT
         ...
 TGT     DC    AL1(*-*),...
```

Do you wonder what possible operations might be executed? Direct use of user-supplied machine operation codes means any computer instruction can be issued. Additionally we have violated reentrancy rules by modifying a program instruction, although this flaw could be corrected by moving TGT to a data area and executing it. Moving TGT to a data area also allows us to support different length instructions, a dangerous generalization. Making our second example reentrant will not help its most serious flaw: mysteriousness. The caller is really given carte blanche, and the code reader is left in the dust.

I know of no techniques for dynamic instruction modification that produce truly readable code. No important compiler language, excepting only list processing languages, includes this ability as a language feature. You will be well to be rid of this technique.

Special Instruction Sets

Avoid using special instruction sets unless you actually need the services they provide. Their use expands your hardware reliability exposure to failures peculiar to the special instruction set. Further, their use reduces program portability, since machine models without the feature cannot process your code.

A former co-worker chose to use *decimal* instructions for counting in a scan routine. One evening, when these failed, the system stopped recognizing JOB cards, knocking it out of service. I didn't like the drive in or the time puzzling over the failing code. I told the skeptical engineer to test the decimal instruction set for a failure and enjoyed his astonished look when the diagnostics backed me up. The machine was out for twelve hours.

However, my enjoyment wasn't worth the drive. Had our code not used packed decimal instructions, my trip would have been unnecessary. Had the failure occurred in code normally associated with the decimal instruction set (COBOL programs, for example), diagnosis would have been much faster. I eventually rewrote the code to use fixed-point instructions.

Of course, if major benefits can be had from using a special instruction set, its use is appropriate. In this case, centralize use of the special instructions into a particular subroutine or macro to ease later conversion to a machine without the feature. However, when standard machine instructions will do the job nearly as well as special ones, use the standard instructions.

Memory Management

The area of memory you select for a modification can affect not only the performance, but the very operation of the modification.

If you are not going to explicitly free the memory, pay particular attention to when the system will free it. End-of-task may be hours later, if the task is a terminal session, or never, if the task is a teleprocessing system. If your change allocates memory repeatedly without freeing, you could run the task out of storage. Personally I prefer to explicitly free memory my programs use instead of relying on the operating system. Explicit freeing helps program readability. Don't leave future readers (perhaps yourself trying to eliminate an out-of-storage condition) wondering when your program is finished using a block of storage.

In MVS systems, memory location can have a dramatic effect on system performance. If every task in your system allocates a new 1000-byte control block, it matters a great deal whether that memory is local to the task's region or in the global common storage area (CSA). Needless or marginal use of CSA can increase system overhead dramatically.

The memory allocation process isn't free. If you have the choice of allocating many small pieces of memory or one larger area, use the latter approach. The strain on both you and the system will be reduced.

Duration of the memory is also a consideration, particularly when adding fields to existing control blocks. A control block that is reallocated before each command is processed would, obviously, be a poor spot to save permanent system status information.

To sum up, compare the duration of your modification with the memory it uses to make certain a good match has been obtained.

Comments in Assembler Language

My commenting techniques have evolved with experience, but I continue to look for improvements. Comments should improve readability; they should showcase the intent of the code for later readers.

At the start of a routine, I code comment cards that tell what the routine does and how each machine register is used. The register list provides a reference during coding that prevents confusion. Later, the register list continues to come in handy.

At major points in the routine, I put in comment cards to explain the milestone, such as finding the control block we are looking for in a chain.

In the right-most columns of each card of a modification, I put a code to indicate the overall modification. (I formerly coded my initials, but the ego-boost of seeing WSM in the code is less helpful than knowing the function the code is to perform.) Some friends of mine include a comment card at the front of the routine dating the modification and explaining its function.

Finally, I include a comment on each line of machine code. This comment should tell more than what the machine instruction will do: it should tell *why*. For example, I tell whether the shift instruction is aligning data or multiplying by a power of two.

Reviewing these different occasions for comments, you can see that several different functions were implemented with the comment instruction. Ideally we would have a like number of different assembler or compiler techniques for commenting, but we don't. Instead we should remember the variety of reasons

136

for coding a comment in a program and be sure the comment reflects its reason for being.

Reviewing the program in the reentrancy chapter, I realized that I had fallen short of my standards. Here is that same program, with improved comments:

SAMPLE COMMENTED REENTRANT PROGRAM

```
*
*         PROGRAM TO FIND AND DISPLAY SYSTEM VERSION
*
*         R1   POINTER TO VERSION IN SYSTEM CVT
*         R2   VERSION FIELD SIZE
*
RENT      CSECT
*
*         ALLOCATE AND PREPARE THE SAVE/WORK AREA
*
          ...                  (save registers)
          GETMAIN RU,LV=WORKSIZE     ALLOCATE WORK AREA
          ...                  (establish new save/work area)
          MVC   WTOTGT(WTOLEN),WTOLIST  COPY WTO LIST
*
*         FIND AND COPY THE SYSTEM VERSION
*
          L     R1,CVTPTR           CVT BASE
          S     R1,=A(CVT-CVTRELNO) BACKUP TO RELEASE NUMBER
          LA    R2,L'CVTRELNO       SET TEXT LENGTH
          EX    R2,COPYTXT          MOVE IN THE TEXT
*
*         DISPLAY THE VERSION INFORMATION
*
          WTO   MF=(E,WTOTGT)       ISSUE WTO
*
*         EXIT, FREEING SAVE/WORK AREA
*
          ...                  (remove save/work area from chain)
          FREEMAIN RU,LV=WORKSIZE,A=(R1)  FREE WORK AREA
          ...                  (return)
*
*         CONSTANTS AND DSECTS
*
```

SAMPLE COMMENTED REENTRANT PROGRAM (Cont.)

```
WTOLIST  WTO    '.... IS THE RELEASE NUMBER',ROUTCDE=(11),MF=L
WTOLEN   EQU    *-WTOLIST
COPYTXT  MVC    WTOTGT+4(*-*),0(R1) COPY TEXT
         LTORG
WORKAREA DSECT
SAVEAREA DS     18F                 SAVE AREA
WTOTGT   DS     (WTOLEN)X           WTO AREA
WORKSIZE EQU    *-WORKAREA          LENGTH OF GETMAIN'D AREA
```

Good comments will help you throughout the life of a program, whether you wish to move on to something else (and therefore need freedom from your product) or if you wish to continue expanding the program.

Eliminate the Diagnostics

Compilers and assemblers often flag code what we write but still produce usable object programs. Although during development we may run those object programs, a program that compiles with diagnostics is not complete. Even if the typos are not serious, they should all be eliminated.

I do *not* stress that, because error message generation is usually a separate phase of compilers and assemblers, eliminating all the causes of diagnostics speeds up compilation. Although true, this argument is a weak reason for cleaning up our syntax errors.

Software lasts longer than we expect. We often continue to use "one shot" programs that are years old. Consider the chilling experience of recompiling or reassembling someone else's old standby and seeing error messages. Is the undefined label error serious? Are we missing part of the program source? How about the warning message from the system macro we invoked? Did that always appear, or is a new version of the macro incompatible with our program? Can we ignore the alignment error, or does it reflect deeper ills in the program? By the way, I don't think that commenting an avoidable compiler or assembler error is a suitable replacement for eliminating the diagnostic.

Once past the language processors, we have another opportunity to leave confusing diagnostics. Unresolved references detected by the linkage editor or loader can be just as baffling as the preceding language problems. Are we missing a critical subroutine, or can we safely ignore the message? Once again, we should not confuse development techniques, which may require running with modules missing, with packaging when we construct a clean system.

Failure to correct the errors reflected by diagnostics leaves haunting questions for future systems programmers, particularly if they can't ask the programmer who originally wrote the routine. Follow the golden rule: *Don't leave a puzzle for the next chap.*

What Version of the Program Is This?

In "Nothing Changed," I discussed making sure you actually install the modification you are testing. You can use many methods to include version information in the program and make it available to the user. Several techniques will be discussed; depending on the application one or more may be suitable. Many later doubts can be prevented by installing version reporting.

Compilers often begin or end the compilation listing with messages that indicate both the version and date of the complier. They and other batch processors may include version information as part of the output page heading. Both methods mark listings so that output from different copies of the program may be recognized.

Interactive programs often have a prompt message:

why not

```
EDIT 3.1 12/1/79
```

instead of

```
EDIT
```

If the increased amount of prompt output is a problem, perhaps it can be produced only when the processor is first invoked.

Whenever I install a new version of JES2, I make it a point to change the separator page slightly from the previous version. Fortunately I receive many suggestions for this. The

141

minor change allows me to quickly recognize under which version of the system a job was run.

We can apply the same principles to program storage. If the assembler can substitute the current date in a text field, we can include this in the *eyecatcher* that begins each module. If not, we can manually code this value, and try to remember to update it. Either way we can determine the vintage of the program directly by examining a storage dump.

By ensuring that your program's output tells its age, you eliminate one guessing game often associated with problem diagnosis.

Follow-up

1. Using the techniques from this section, preferably with the checklist from Appendix B in front of you, code an assembler language program. If you assume that a code inspection will follow, do you find yourself taking more care of details?

2. To what extent does "Structured Programming" reduce the need for "Comments" in a program?

3. Write an automatic program examination routine using the tests in "Smelling Dead Fish" and inspect a few programs you have. Do programs that have caused you trouble score high on the two tests mentioned?

SECTION 5

Keeping It Symbolic

Assembler language programs are extremely difficult to modify. Fortunately there are techniques that ease the pain of program modification. Our goal is to avoid making anything about the program more specific than necessary. All of the techniques in this section reduce *hard-wiring* in the program, so that we will be able to adapt it more easily.

The Current Location Counter,*

The current location counter "*" can be a big help or a serious problem, depending on usage. Some time back, I was performing maintenance on a software product and discovered problems with a particular function. When I examined the failing routine, I discovered that a few instructions were being skipped with the assembler instruction:

```
BE   *+36
```

A little further detective work disclosed that between * and +36 (many lines later) subsequent maintenance, applied out of sequence, had added instructions and changed where +36 referred. I was lucky: +36 referred to the middle of an instruction and caused a program check. Often such an error will instead point to the start of the wrong instruction, and mysterious failures will occur because certain instructions are either executed or omitted incorrectly. Certainly failing to apply an update was our error, but such a large relative offset is an accident looking for a chance to happen.

If the machine instructions vary in length, as on the System/370, instead of having fixed size, as on the IBM 7040, determining relative offsets is even harder. One has to total the lengths of the individual instructions to be skipped, instead of just counting them. If maintenance changes the length of a single skipped instruction, the branch enters the middle of an instruction and likely will exit with a program check. As the number

147

of instructions skipped increases, so does the chance of error. (For more on counting errors, see "Don't Count Characters.")

Labels are free, and can easily be created as needed. Cleverly chosen, they add to program documentation.† They provide much more flexibility than relative locations. When relative offsets get into double digits (*+10), use a label instead. (When switching machines, be careful of whether the current location counter points to the start or to the end of the current instruction. This varies with manufacturers. IBM's location counter points to the start of the current instruction.) Maybe we should never use relative locations.

---

†But see Gerald M. Weinberg, *The Psychology of Computer Programming* (New York: Van Nostrand, 1971), pp. 162–64. Weinberg points out that mnemonic labels can be dangerous if they don't agree with program function or if they confuse the reader.

Mapping Macros

Programs access control blocks by two common techniques. In the first, you look up the offsets needed and code them into the program. To use the second, include the necessary mapping macros from system libraries in the program and code the names of the fields to be referenced.

I strongly recommend the second method. The offsets of fields in control blocks are not physical constants; they change with some frequency. Mapping macros allow the program to change with the control block and are good warning devices if the field involved has disappeared. They enhance program documentation. Absolute offsets offer none of these features. They don't even appear in the program cross-reference!

A relative of the first technique is often observed when many copies of a control block must be built. A skeleton of the control block is constructed with define constant (DC) assembler operations, and moved wholesale into the control block being built. After the move, particular fields are set using mapping macro offsets. This technique is dangerous. If the mapping macro changes, the constant skeleton remains the same, and misaligned information will be loaded into the control block. The errors can be subtle and thus difficult to detect and isolate. Better to have used mapping macros either by writing instructions to set each field specifically or by building the skeleton using the field offsets.

Using absolute offsets constitutes going into business for yourself. A friend of mine described a bizarre form of this activity: "An inexperienced programmer decided that the system macro instructions produced assembler language code that was too inefficient for his program. He laboriously replaced the macro calls with hand coded, optimized versions of the expansions. The program worked properly for a while. Unfortunately, after the programmer had moved on, new releases of the operating system brought with them revised system macros, reflecting system interface changes. The optimized program stopped working altogether, and other programmers had to modify the thing to use the system macros again.'' The required modifications, essentially redoing the programmer's work, undoubtedly cost more than the ''optimization'' saved.

Mapping macros are not unique to assembler languages; the COBOL INCLUDE statement and PL/I's preprocessor both support their use. A friend of mine used concatenated DD statements to build input to the FORTRAN compiler which included a standard set of COMMON block definitions. Use mapping macros whenever you can and you will save considerable checking and correcting later on.

Device Dependency

Operating systems and access methods relieve the computer user of concerns about the characteristics of devices being used. Unfortunately not all systems programmers have gotten the word.

Far too many programs have hard-coded tables that contain, for example, the number of tracks per cylinder or the English name corresponding to a numeric device type. Only devices known at the time the table is coded are supported. When a new device arrives, someone must find and rework all such tables to support it. If many programs use this method, the unexpected conversion is painful.

When I discover a table like this, I replace it with a call to the appropriate system routine,† which determines what the value should be. Here's an example of OS/VS device independent coding:

DEVICE INDEPENDENT CODING EXAMPLE

```
*
*
*       TRACKS PER CYLINDER AND DEVICE TYPE DISPLAY ROUTINE
*       ALL DEVICES SUPPORTED BY OS ARE SUPPORTED.
*
*       INPUT = POINTER TO TIOT ENTRY IN R5
*
*       OUTPUT = WTO MESSAGE DDNAME,
*                DEVICE NAME, AND TRACKS PER CYLINDER
*
```

---

†For OS/VS, see "Obtaining I/O Device Characteristics" in the chapter entitled, "System Macro Instructions," in *OS/VS2 System Programming Library: Data Management*, IBM, form C26-3830.

151

DEVICE INDEPENDENT CODING EXAMPLE (Cont.)

```
*          DATA USED: UCB, TIOT
*
*          REGISTERS USED:
*
*          R0    DEVNAMET MODULE ADDRESS, DEVNAMET LOOP LIMIT
*          R1    WORK, DEVNAMET INDEX
*          R2    UCB POINTER
*          R5    TIOT ENTRY POINTER
*          R12   RETURN ADDRESS
*
BLOCKS     DS     0H
           SLR    R2,R2               CLEAR FOR INSERT
           ICM    R2,7,TIOEFSRT       GET DD'S FIRST UCB PTR
           BZ     NOUCB               DD HAS NO UCB -- IGNORE
           USING  UCRCMSEG,R2         TELL ASMFX
*
*                 IS THIS A DIRECT ACCESS DEVICE?
*
           TM     UCBDVCLS,UCB3DACC   DIRECT ACCESS DEVICE?
           BO     ISDA                NO, ISSUE MSG
NOUCB      MVC    WTOAREA(BADLEN),MSGBAD   COPY BASE MESSAGE
           MVC    WTOAREA+BADDD(8),TIOEDDNM   COPY DDNAME
           WTO    MF=(E,WTOAREA)      ISSUE THE MESSAGE
           BR     R12
*
*                 ASK MVS FOR DEVICE DATA, FORMAT TRACKS/CYL
*
ISDA       MVC    WTOAREA(GOODLEN),MSGGOOD
           DEVTYPE TIOEDDNM,DTWORK,DEVTAB   GET DEVICE DATA
           LH     R1,DTWORK+10        GET TRACKS/CYL
           CVD    R1,DOUBLE           CONVERT TO PACKED
           MVC    WTOAREA+MSGTRKS(4),EDITMSK   MOVE IN EDIT MASK
           ED     WTOAREA+MSGTRKS(4),DOUBLE+6   EDIT IN COUNT
*
*                 LOAD DEVICE NAME TABLE IF NEEDED
*
           L      R1,DEVTAB           DEVICE NAME TABLE
           LTR    R1,R1               LOADED?
           BNZ    SEARCH              YES
           LOAD   EP=DEVNAMET         NO, LOAD IT
           LR     R1,R0               MAKE ADDRESSABLE
           ST     R0,DEVTAB           SAVE IT
*
*                 FIND THE PROPER DEVICE NAME
*
SEARCH     L      R0,0(,R1)           GET COUNT
           LA     R1,4(,R1)           SET FIRST ENTRY
NEXTDEV    CLC    UCBTBYT3(2),10(R1)  MATCH?
           BE     DEVMATCH            YES.
```

DEVICE INDEPENDENT CODING EXAMPLE (Cont.)

```
          LA    R1,12(,R1)              BUMP DEV NAME COUNTER
          BCT   R0,NEXTDEV              AND KEEP AT IT
          LA    R1,=CL8'UNKNOWN'        SHOW UNKNOWN DEVICE
*
*               MOVE DEVICE NAME TO MSG AND RETURN
*
DEVMATCH  MVC   WTOAREA+DEVID(8),0(R1)  COPY DEVICE NAME
          MVC   WTOAREA+GOODDD(8),TIOEDDNM  COPY DDNAME
          WTO   MF=(E,WTOAREA)          ACTUALLY TYPE THE MESSAGE
          BR    R12

MSGGOOD   WTO   'DDNAME.. IS A ........ AND HAS NNNN TRKS/CYL',    C
                ROUTCDE=(11),MF=L
MSGTRKS   EQU   *-17-MSGGOOD,4
DEVID     EQU   4+14,8
GOODDD    EQU   4
GOODLEN   EQU   *-MSGGOOD
MSGBAD    WTO   'DDNAME.. IS NOT DIRECT ACCESS',                  C
                ROUTCDE=(11),MF=L
BADDD     EQU   4
BADLEN    EQU   *-MSGBAD
EDITMSK   DC    X'40202120'
          LTORG

WORKAREA  DSECT
SAVEAREA  DS    18F
DOUBLE    DS    D
DEVTAB    DS    F
DTWORK    DS    5F
WTOAREA   DS    CL(BADLEN)
          ORG   WTOAREA
          DS    CL(GOODLEN)
          ORG   ,
          DS    0D                      ALIGNMENT
WORKLEN   EQU   *-WORKAREA
A         CSECT
          PRINT    NOGEN
TIOT      DSECT
          IEFTIOT1
          IEFUCBOB
          IHAPSA
          END
```

Although writing generalized, device independent coding may take more of my time than simply adding or changing an entry in a table, it will reduce (possibly to zero) the time necessary to support the *next* new device.

Don't Count Characters

When forming text strings for messages, avoid counting the characters. Let the machine do the counting, and you will code more quickly.

use this

```
        MVC   0(L'MSG,R1),MSG
        LA    R1,L'MSG(R1)        BUMP TEXT POINTER
        . . .
MSG     DC    C'JOB NOT FOUND FOR YOUR USERID'
```

not this

```
        MVC   0(28,R1),=C'JOB NOT FOUND FOR YOUR USERID'
        LA    R1,28(R1)         BUMP TEXT POINTER
```

Both examples move the message into the buffer area pointed to by register 1 and then update register 1. Although the second example requires more typing initially, the assembler supplies the length, so you don't have to. Better still, if you must change the message, as is often the case, only the message text need be changed. The assembler adjusts the length references automatically.

Eliminating errors is an even more compelling reason for letting the computer do the counting. Psychological research shows that human short-term memory is "seven plus or minus two† digits." Thus, an eleven-digit phone number is difficult to remember, while recalling a seven-digit phone number is relatively easy. A similar principle applies to counting characters; above about seven, errors creep in. To demonstrate this, the length in the second example is incorrect. Can you determine whether the count is high or low, and by how many? How often during debugging have you seen messages with garbage embedded or characters missing, due to bad counts?

A one-character length error isn't critical for the preceding error message, but imagine the effect on the message:

```
HIGHEST RETURN CODE = 08
```

Losing the last character completely changes the meaning of the message from bad news (RC=8) to good news (RC=0).

Counting characters should remind us of the monks drawing the illuminated manuscripts. Hours of time are spent counting, recounting, and correcting the counts. The large amount of labor does nothing to improve the product.

In the mid 1960s, the staff of the University of Pennsylvania Computer Center modified the IBM 7040 FORTRAN compiler to support string quotes in FORMAT statements. Management had discovered that errors counting characters accounted for a staggering proportion of all errors made by users and took action to eliminate the problem. Only an accident of historic timing kept string quotes out of the ANSI 1966 FORTRAN standard. Compilers that offered the feature began appearing shortly after the standard was issued‡. Fortunately the newer standards include the facility.

When you count characters, you are picking up work the computer can do better. Your program cannot have fewer errors if you count characters, at best it can only have as many. Let the computer do this chore.

---

†For more details, see George A. Miller, "The Magical Number Seven, Plus or Minus Two: Some Limits on our Capacity for Processing Information," *Psychological Review* 63 (1956), pp. 81–97.

‡Private communication with Martin Greenfield of Honeywell.

Assembly Parameters

Many second-generation and early third-generation software systems use assembly parameters to support options. This method saves main storage by eliminating code not chosen at assembly time. Unfortunately this savings has a high price.

Obviously, to change assembly parameters the program must be reassembled. For the user, the time and cost involved make experimenting with system options inconvenient. If changing a single switch takes a half hour of processing, the user will be reluctant to try the change.

This same inconvenience hurts the developer as well. Rigorous testing of a program with assembly parameters demands using all possible versions of the program. Even if only binary parameters are used, the number of different versions rapidly becomes intolerable: a program with only ten parameters requires over a thousand ($2^{10} = 1024$) test versions!

How else can we tailor our system to user requirements? Instead of using assembly parameters, read an intialization file and build an options work area to save the options. Thus, you need merely stop and restart your system to change options. To reduce the main storage costs, break the system into modules by function and do not load unused modules.

Follow-up

1. Again, take an existing program of yours, and review it for generality. How well does the code follow the suggestions in this section, and how well does the program accept changes?

2. Review production disk support programs at your installation (such as the direct access space billing program and the utility space cleaning program) to determine how device independent they are.

SECTION 6

Testing

Once the code is written, we must determine if it functions properly. The following tips should help you select tests that will bear fruit.

Generally, the problem with testing is not so much with quantity of testing as with quality: if the same test case is run through a program a million times, you don't learn much from the last 999,999 passes. You will get more mileage out of using a variety of data values within the normal and invalid ranges of the program. Careful selection of test cases and methods is the key. Volume can get in the way; if you run a million passes, you cannot manually check a million lines of output. For volume testing, automatic output comparator programs are infinitely more reliable than people for reading the output.†

When we code a program, we work long and hard at planning how to make the program work. For testing we must reverse our thinking and devote just as much thought and energy to disproving our idea that the program is working. Only once we have tried earnestly to disprove the program's proper operation can we begin to believe that it works properly. Successful runs do not increase our confidence; only the mass of test cases, each designed to induce a failure, each passed sucessfully, do.

---

†Paul Heckel, "A Technique for Isolating Differences Between Files," *Communications of the ACM* 21, no. 4 (April 1978), pp. 264–8, discusses general techniques for writing file comparison programs.

Much of the time we take to develop a program is spent testing to see if it works. We can choose testing methods that detect more errors and do so more rapidly with the techniques that follow.

Planning the Test

In systems programming, tests are generally a lot of trouble. Often, stand-alone machine time or a special setup is necessary. In a situation where at best one hour of machine time a day was available for testing (and more likely only a half hour), I discovered that my daily productivity depended strictly on the productivity of the test shot.

I adopted the practice of preparing a detailed test plan ahead of time. I did everything I could to make myself ready to test, preparing datasets, card decks, and test cases. I wrote a detailed schedule of actions, to ensure that a key test would not be forgotten in the heat of battle. I began getting done what I wanted to in my test time, and I could make use of the abbreviated test time that was sometimes handed to me, because I needed very little preparatory time.

161

The effectiveness of NASA's manned space program was due in part to similar practices. The agenda for each space flight was drilled repeatedly until the men knew exactly what they were to do during the mission. The technique works as well for me as it did for them.

The Quick Test

Prior to production operation, a modified system must pass a standard test. Our objective in this test is to detect and eliminate glaring errors in new software prior to installation.

Speed is a prime consideration for this test; total time must be short enough that running the test is less trouble than explaining why you didn't. A total run time of no more than ten to twenty minutes is required. Although an eight-hour test might give us more assurance, such a test is much more difficult to schedule and check.

The test would include specific checks for problems that historically have been overlooked and not caught. As a first cut, I would recommend including batch jobs that spool a moderate amount of regular and special forms output and a terminal session, using an automatic script to eliminate timing differences associated with different testers' typing skills.

The results would be checked automatically: the tests themselves would report success or failure. Following this, a short accounting run would examine the cost of the test and compare this with a prestored standard, perhaps with some tolerance factor (1 percent?) included. (I suggest an accounting run because one common effect of bad system changes is bad accounting information.)

A friend of mine, charged with compiler maintenance at a shop, collected disasters. He had a box of 1000 cards of programs that caused failures in the compiler and he ran this against every new version of the compiler. As new releases improved the product, fewer of the jobs took out the compiler. His assortment of tests took under a minute to execute and print, and it was easy to tell how well the new compiler did on his benchmark.

Although such a test will not provide complete assurance, for maintenance changes, the new system will be examined in a repeatable fashion. We are stealing a medical technique here: when I visit my doctor, my blood pressure, weight, and pulse are always checked, regardless of the reason for my visit. The quick test does the same for our operating system.

Test the Original Function

When we add a feature to existing system code, we must take care that our elbows don't inadvertently damage it. We perform regression testing.

A while back, some associates of mine implemented a fast turnaround service. They wanted to limit the fast turnaround jobs to 30 seconds of wall-clock time, no tape or disk mounts, and no allocation recovery. They modified the HASP adaptive dispatcher to limit the jobs to the time decided, and the OS allocation routines were changed to fail the jobs rather than perform the mounts.

Although different individuals wrote the modifications, there was a striking similarity in post-implementation problems. Once the HASP modification was installed, the adaptive dispatcher no longer selected input/output limited jobs ahead of compute bound jobs. Once the mount change was installed, allocation recovery always failed!

The unintentional destruction of these two important system functions was completely preventable. When a modification to an existing program is made, the program's original function *must* be tested to see if it still happens to work. Failure to check (and both implementers were guilty) can mean that bad work gets out the door. A ready package of tests (perhaps those used to validate the software originally, or see "The Quick Test") reduces developer reluctance towards regression testing. Test size can be a problem, but review of the modification can suggest small tests of the functions most likely to be affected by the change. Success with these tests will increase our confidence.

Retesting

Once a program bug has been found and corrected, the correction must be tested to ensure proper operation. At least the same tests that detected the error must be rerun. Depending on the magnitude of the correction, even more testing may be required.

Our intent here partly is to slow down the debugging process and increase the thought that goes into debugging. When we find an error, we should consider if global tendencies are implied: was the same mistake made throughout the module? If so, we shouldn't just correct the first occurrence. Don't take nine runs to correct the same semantic error on nine different control cards; get them all the first time.

Unless program modification is approached as if any change will probably be incorrect, the change has little chance of success. No change is so small as to be exempted from retesting.

Fast Clocks and Counters

Sometimes we combine timers and counters to individually control many activities on the computer. To ease debugging problems, change the counts and timers involved so that, for example, the fifteen minute delay envisioned in the final version occurs in a minute and a half on the test version. Just as model railroaders compensate for their short mainlines with fast clocks, we can compensate for our short test shots.

I cannot resist including an anecdote here. A friend was developing TSO inactivity logoff and complained to me that he had gotten very little done in his half-hour test shots while waiting out the fifteen minutes. I recommended that he try a much shorter interval and thus allow himself many more trials per test shot. (I had had good luck with this technique.) He liked the idea and immediately began testing that way. Another friend attempted to use TSO during the other's test and still remembers the increase in his productivity that the frequent SESSION CANCELLED messages spurred him to!

This is the same logic we apply to testing system limits: instead of testing the maximum output lines limit with 100,000-line jobs, we set the limit lower (like 1000 lines) and use jobs that exceed that lower limit.

A danger with a fast clock or counter is that quirks of the standard situation will not become evident during the fast tests. A real-time final test is essential.

Restrictive Environments

It seems obvious that a program must be tested in the most hostile environment possible. Choosing that environment takes some care.

If a program is to run on both 360 and 370 systems, each running under OS/MVT, the 360 is the more restrictive machine, as unaligned operands are not supported, and attempts to use them win program checks.

If the program is to run on both OS/MVT on a 360 and an OS/VS system on a 370, then both environments are restrictive, and both must be tested. The VS environment offers many more opportunities for memory protection violations, because a greater percentage of memory is fetch protected or undefined.

Test under every restrictive environment the program is expected to face.

Test Every Branch

The ideal for debugging is to test every path through the program. Unfortunately this usually means an astronomically large set of combinations.

I try to test both paths from every conditional branch I code. I attempt to generate every error message I invent, and enter every error exit I code. If the exit is normally entered only after peculiar events, such as hardware errors, I will force entry using an absolute patch.

Decision tables, because they list all of your test conditions, provide valuable assistance when preparing test cases. They come in handy again when diagnosing failures; if you know which actions were not taken, you can determine which rules are failing, and therefore which conditions are not properly tested. Structured programming reduces the number of branches in a program, which thus reduces the number of tests required. If you test both sides of every branch you code, obvious errors in the code will be flushed out.

What we are getting into here are test cases and test data. Test cases should be chosen to test every operating range of the program. For example, we modified JES2 to support a wider range of remote numbers: instead of 1–255, we allow 1–999. Because internally the storage format went from a byte to a halfword, testing was necessary using a remote in the old range (1–255) and one in the extended range (256–999) to confirm proper operation. Some test cases from outside the proper operating range were also be used to ensure recognition of improper data.

When selecting test cases for numeric values, select values close to the boundaries of the data range. A friend explained a bug in some code that allocated disk space: normally the user specified the number of cylinders needed (range 1–99) and the system allocated that amount. The code had been tested for the bottom of the range (1–5) but not towards the top (99, 100). When a user asked for ten cylinders, and the program converted this number to a hexadecimal value (A) and passed it on to a service routine, which expected input in decimal and could not process the hexadecimal request. The code had been working "successfully" for some time because most users only wanted between one and nine cylinders. Testing the extremes of the data range would have flushed this error.

A successful test data file contains an assortment of test cases, valid and invalid. The file is not so large that it takes forever to run or produces so much output that the results cannot be checked.

A co-worker once remarked of a project in which he had been involved that debugging was very difficult because it took a half hour to load the data for the test, and often the test would abort shortly thereafter. In that sort of situation, paring down the test file would have accelerated testing considerably.

Remember, we are trying to follow many paths through the program, rather than following the same path with many different data values. The issue is not whether the machine can multiply correctly, but whether our program logic is correct and appropriate.

Stress Testing

System software usually relies on certain resources to operate properly. When these resources are unavailable, the software should slow down, perhaps even stop. System failures should not be a direct consequence of resource shortages, however.

We test the system for survival of these conditions by inducing them. Detune the system to induce the shortage: if we normally operate with 100 buffers, set up for operation with ten. Fill the disk files completely and see how the system runs. We expect to see sluggish response, long delays, and perhaps stoppages. If instead loops or program checks occur, debugging is indicated.

The other side of the coin, low system load also deserves some attention. Sometimes systems operating under unusually light workloads show peculiar error conditions. Incorrect synchronization may be reflected in long delays during light load conditions.

The code to handle resource shortages or an idle machine, in a properly tuned and well-used system, is seldom exercised, so special care must be taken to ensure its proper operation.

Data File Acceptance Testing

Generally, unlike applications programs, which process user-supplied data files, systems programs use data files they previously created, so that data file compatibility and accuracy problems are well controlled. We should not allow this norm to confuse us when a data file is manufactured externally to the program and programmer that will use it. Even if our best friend is to create the file, we must take some precautions to ensure quality and our understanding of the file's format. We write special routines to examine the data file prior to using it on our system.

Range Checking

When the file is delivered, each record should be checked to ensure that the data items are each within the appropriate range. For example, if a field indicates sex, only M, F, and perhaps "unknown" are acceptable. If a field contains a social security number, only numerics will do. If information is written in bundles composed, for example, of one header record followed by ten detail records, check to ensure that the entire file conforms to this standard. Extraordinary tests, too time-consuming for the production system, may be performed since our range checking program run needn't operate interactively.

Frequency Distributions

Once we know that the fields in the file all have the proper format, we may proceed to more subtle testing. For major fields, build a frequency distribution of values for the field. As usual, we are looking for a bell curve. For a local mailing list, zip codes should cluster around our own. Records corresponding to points outside the curve should be examined. This technique is similar to the range checking, but with human assistance.

Sorts

Sort the file by each major field and list the first few (2 percent?) and last few records in the sorted output. This will cull invalid special characters and inappropriate leading blanks in the fields.

Redundancy

Sometimes the data will include some natural redundancy which may be used to advantage. In mailing lists, the City, State Zip Code data is usually stored. For each group with the same zip code, compare the City, State field. If all but one address with a zip code of 22043 has the post office name Falls Church, VA, and one has Fairfax, VA, flag the exception record.

Statistical Techniques

For a larger file, it may be appropriate to extract a random sample of the file and check it manually against the source data.†

---

†See William G. Cochran, *Sampling Techniques*, 3d. ed. (New York: Wiley, 1977) for a complete treatment of statistical sampling.

The sample's error frequency tells us the overall quality of the file. Care must be taken to choose an appropriate sample size and to sample the right population. If the file contains, for example, both customers and local internal users and is to be used to mail information, then we would probably want to take a random sample of the customer records only, as the internal users are all in the same building and errors aren't so critical.

Data files deserve the same scrutiny as the programs that use them. Data file acceptance testing can confirm our understanding of the file format and assure us of file quality well before the system is operational.

Methodic Testing

Testing by parties independent of the program's authors sheds a different light on system function. This testing is not a substitute for testing by the authors; it follows successful system checkout.

The work is assigned by providing the tester with a copy of the program documentation and whatever equipment (keypunch, terminal, or perhaps operator console) one uses to access the system. Note that two disciplines are forced on the developers: they must *have* a users' manual, and they must have a working copy of the system available. By satisfying these requirements, we pass an important milestone.

The tester then proceeds to use every system command and function, to try out *everything* the manual says the system will do. The tests are not performed in the order shown in the manual, some of the tests are performed twice, and some things the manual says the system won't do are also attempted. We hope that this proves to be boring work, that every function and option will check out, that the output will always match expectations. Usually, however, problems are flushed out during the testing. Testing *scripts,* preprogrammed input streams used by the batch or terminal system, can eliminate much of the tediousness of this sort of testing.

System Testing

Once the programmers and testers agree that the new system works properly, further testing may still be indicated. Here are some ways to get the most out of the system test.

Free Computer Time

A service bureau can repeatedly produce a heavy test load on the new system by offering the system free of charge. The benefits of this technique include a heavy system load and a variety of test cases mimicking the system's eventual real environment. Such tests tend to be good public relations, almost regardless of how well the tested system runs. The free time cushions the trauma of errors in the new system.

Simulators

A variety of hardware and software techniques allow a heavy terminal user load, a heavy batch load, or nonexistent devices to be simulated. A heavy system load can be induced, but the simulator is usually only as creative as the *scripts*, or lists of commands, the simulated users follow. The unpredictability of real users is not so easy to simulate.

Bounties

During testing for a security system, one organization offered a reward of a few dollars for any successful breach of the system. The tester works more diligently when a financial reward is offered. The effort expended may be disproportionately large compared with the reward because the satisfaction of such rewards often exceeds their actual worth.

Ego Appeal

"Only the best, most sophisticated users get to use the new system in this early state of development," says the system developer, and user is off and running. Play on the pride of your users.

Reviewing these techniques, we see one that relies on a special program or system, and three that simulate the testers to do a more diligent job. If you consider system testing within this framework, other methods should occur to you.

Follow-up

1. Survey what test methods your installation uses for small and large system changes. Are any of the methods previously discussed used?

2. Assume that management is about to require use of the previously described testing technique that you like least. Develop reasons for not standardizing that method.

Management

I had hoped to avoid including a classification of debugging topics entitled "other" or "etc.," but some important issues are more global than even the design techniques mentioned in the "Prevention" section. The following discussion relates to management and professionals' attitudes more than specific methods, such as avoiding unconditional branches.

Although these topics are less "firm" than, say, those in the "Coding Practices" section, they are just as important, perhaps more so. The attitudes we have about our work are a significant factor in how the work is performed; we should not neglect them.

System Documentation

Systems programmers often skimp on detailed design documentation. The average tenure of employees with an organization in the industry is about two years. Since software tends to live longer than it should, personnel changes make whatever documentation gets written all the more valuable. You cannot always ask the original programmer.

I encourage programmers to document by allowing documentation in whatever form the programmer feels would be most appropriate and by allowing sufficient project time for the documentation to be written.

I have seen so many beautifully written outlines for documentation that I no longer put any faith in them. (I have never seen more than one document following the outline, and none written by someone other than the outline's author.) Channel the time the programmer would have spent resisting the documentation standard into writing nonstandard documentation. A document in the hand is worth ten standards in the bush. If you have to choose, remember that documentation of the data formats is more critical than documentation of the code.

When preparing or reviewing documentation, remember that a program that is difficult to document is also poorly designed. If the effort required to document the module is excessive, perhaps we need a new module, not a technical writer.

Scheduling walkthroughs during development is a cunning way to stimulate documentation. Few folks enjoy getting up before a group and saying, "Um, er, well, ..." Prior preparation and distribution of handouts for the walkthrough will further improve the walkthrough.

181

User Group Meetings

A good way to stay on top of a given piece of software is to attend the appropriate user group meetings. For medium and large IBM systems, GUIDE and SHARE come to mind.† It seems that any program, package, or machine with more than a dozen users has a users' group. The amount of free help available at these sessions is staggering. With just 35 people, each with three years of time on the product, you are surrounded by a *century* of experience, ready for your call. If these arguments don't persuade your management to send you to a conference, show them the following:

> The author of this book urges you to invest in your systems programmer: allow him or her to attend the next possible user group meeting. Require him or her to commit to writing a trip report as described under the "Conference Trip Report" chapter as a condition for future conference attendance.

How do you get started with a user group? Join a project. Offer to give a talk about your work or chair a session at the

---

†Both organizations' headquarters are located at One Illinois Center, 111 East Wacker Drive, Chicago, IL 60601.

next conference. Often projects include more listeners than talkers, and the willing worker is welcomed with open arms.

You must be cautious, however, with modifications received through user groups. The modifications exchanged are often very specific, and therefore have shortcomings that the author is unaware of, but that can cause other users considerable trouble. Look these gift horses in the mouth. I do exchange modifications, but carefully. I read exchanged modifications to understand how they work. I subject them to the same thorough test procedure as my own code.

This makes exchanging modifications sound pretty negative and dangerous. The practices described have allowed me to install exchanged modifications with confidence and success, and have reduced the amount of design, coding, and test work I have had to do. This alternative to ignoring anything "not invented here" or relying on the work of others without test should improve your productivity as well.

Between the information available at the conference and the modifications you can borrow, you will discover that the cost of traveling to the conference and the time you spend there are rapidly paid back in better information about the work you are doing.

Conference Trip Report

Once you attend a conference you will probably want to go to another. How can you encourage your management to invest the money necessary to send you again? I use my trip report to communicate the importance of the meeting to the company.

The trip report should emphasize your company's main interests. Take notes at the sessions you attend. The sessions that apply to your primary job assignment should be given good coverage in the report. If you get something important done at the conference, such as finding something or someone you have been looking for, mention that. If you learn about something important that your organization (although not necessarily you) is or will soon be involved in, mention that.

During World War II, Winston Churchill required that any report he received begin with an abstract, under a page long, to tell him whether he needed to read the report. A similar technique will further improve your trip report. Once the report is drafted, review it for the most significant items from the conference. You should probably find between three and six. Describe them briefly, in order of importance to the company, on the abstract page. Below that, on this same page, include a table of contents for the trip report, so that one needn't read the entire document to find a specific item of interest.

Managers frequently feel uncomfortable around technicians who use vocabulary ("buzz words") not familiar to them. Especially in writing, you should never pass up an opportunity to show yourself as a clarifier, rather than a complicater, before management. Be especially careful about the abstract's readability.

By orienting the trip report towards your company's objectives, and putting a one-page road map on the front, you will communicate the importance of the conference to your management. You will also show your understanding of your company's objectives.

System Integrity

If you have an MVS system (or another operating system with integrity designed in), and your management supports serious system integrity, you will replace open-ended SVCs that negate system security with routines to perform specific functions. Earlier operating systems, such as OS/MFT, OS/MVT, and SVS have countless integrity exposures, some nearly impossible to close, while in MVS, as supplied from IBM, the known integrity exposures have been designed out.

You need management support because tough decisions must be made. A customer who wants you to install a new SVC routine, without examination, modification, or review, must be told no. Management must be willing to back up this position, as integrity is an all-or-nothing condition. The resulting system limits unauthorized experimentation, but that's what you want!

Care must be taken to write SVCs that do not inadvertently provide loopholes. Typical of these loopholes are "address vector problems" and "parameter list problems."

In address vector problems, the SVC transfers control in privileged state to an address provided by the user. In parameter list problems, the SVC stores or fetches in privileged state, using an address supplied by the user. In both cases, validity checking of the user-supplied input is required to prevent the problem. The code must distinguish between a legitimate OS/VS control block and a counterfeit one manufactured by the user.

True system integrity required more work than the simple protection against inadvertent damage that I describe in the chapter called "SVC 255."†

---

†Further information on system integrity can be found in the chapter titled "System Integrity" in *OS/VS2 System Programming Library: Supervisor*, IBM, form C28–0628 and W. S. McPhee, "Operating System Integrity in OS/VS2," *IBM Systems Journal*, Vol. 13, No. 3, 1974, pp. 230–252. IBM's position on MVS integrity is detailed in "Statement of OS/VS2(MVS) System Integrity," a Programming Announcement available from IBM.

Fear of Falling

I have focused on technical approaches that improve our accuracy. Systems programming is an exacting business. For operating systems to show the reliability they do, an incredibly high percentage of the coding must be right. I believe computer programmers have developed incorrect perceptions to help them deal with the demands of the business. Unfortunately these perceptions limit reliability. To get past these limitations, we must first understand where they came from. Bear with me, and I will show you why I believe this.

Almost every systems programmer I know considers himself or herself to be in the top 25 percent of the profession. They reflect this with pride in their prowess in assembler language coding, and in recognizing where an instruction or a byte of storage might be saved. Being able to beat compiler written code is also important. (See the "Making it Beautiful" chapter.) Unfortunately, along the way a lot of grossly inefficient, or worse, incorrect code gets written. We don't really all fit into the top quarter of our profession.

When the 7040 WATFOR† compiler first appeared at the University of Pennsylvania, I noticed a curious phenomenon. Not everyone fell in love with the compiler. Many who might have benefited from it ignored it. Some rationalized that their problem required more efficient compiled code (rephrased, the

---

†WATFOR, a fast FORTRAN compiler, has been supplanted by WATFIV which is available from the University of Waterloo, Dept. of Computing Services, Waterloo, Ontario, Canada, N2L 3G1.

wrong answer had to be computed quickly) provided by the IBM FORTRAN, others complained that some reprogramming was necessary to use WATFOR (rephrased, they were already finding bugs so quickly a compiler couldn't help them). These arguments were true in detail, but false in principle. I believe some programmers don't care for a compiler that catches them exceeding a subscript, or using an uninitialized variable.

At a seminar I attended, *bebugging*,† was discussed. Bebugging allows us to determine the effectiveness of the testing: if you installed 100 bugs, and testing disclosed three, how comfortable do you feel about proceeding to install the system? I found the reactions of the seminar participants quite puzzling: many became most upset at the idea of installing a failure in the system. Admittedly it does run against the grain; I spend enormous amounts of my time finding and eliminating, rather than installing bugs. However, I wonder if something more is involved. Maybe my colleagues know how bad their testing is, and fear so graphic a demonstration.

Management sometimes gets into the act:

> "How was the system test?"
> "We encountered no problems."

Is that good or bad news? I am more comfortable with a test in which some problems are disclosed. The absence of failures may reflect more on the weakness of the testing than the strength of the system, but what is management hoping for? Are we still killing the messenger of doom?

I believe that we react to the exacting demands of our computers with a combination of narcissism and cover-up. The narcissism blinds us, and the cover-up prevents our examining our errors thoroughly.

We cannot prevent or correct our errors by ignoring them. We must assume that errors are present in our work, and subject it to rigorous tests. We must be willing to use the tools that are available and invent new ones as needed to do the job properly.

---

†Installing preplanned bugs in a program or system prior to testing; first described by Gerald M. Weinberg, *The Psychology of Computer Programming* (New York: Van Nostrand, 1971), p. 248. Tom Gilb, *Software Metrics* (Cambridge, Mass.: Winthrop Publishers, 1977), pp. 26–49, includes a good explanation of the method.

Making It Beautiful

The experienced systems programmer may suffer the tendency to replace functioning code with new code, far more sophisticated than the original code, at great cost to overall project schedules. Although overengineering is sometimes appropriate, you should suspect an occupational disease.

"If it works, don't fix it!" If the code involved functions properly and performs at an acceptable speed, then don't touch it.

Replacing a tape read routine to support several new input formats differs from replacing the routine with a new one that uses the translation instruction. The performance improvement had better be dramatic if no external enhancements are accomplished. If the new routine doesn't work, the performance improvements it offers are unimportant.

I mean to distinguish between changes that improve maintainability and prevent future troubles, which you should pursue, and changes intended strictly to make the program faster or more elegant, which you should probably defer. The Boy Scouts have a principle: leave the campsite neater than when you came, to make up for the little untidiness you have probably inadvertently left. Note that they *don't* relandscape the campsite to suit their tastes, however.

Limit your programming effort to that required to do the job. Remember, a good programmer writes debugged assembler language code at a rate of ten lines a day. Note, I said debugged. If you work fifteen-hour days, the rate probably drops to eight, especially if your project is running late. Generally, required changes are tough enough without picking fights.

Project Planning

During conversion to MVS, I had a very positive experience with project planning.† I broke down the JES2 tasks to be done enough to distinguish among one-line changes, less than ten-line changes, larger known scope changes, and major new changes. I allocated times of two days, one week, three weeks, and six weeks, respectively, to these activities, and found that we had enough work in the conversion effort for three people, instead of the one person we had initially projected.

We corrected the major staffing deficit, and the JES2 activity was completed with the rest of the conversion. Without the larger staffing, JES2 conversion would have delayed the MVS conversion.

The absolute accuracy of my estimates is less important than the early recognition of a "Mission Impossible." Early recognition allowed us to take timely corrective actions. The opposite effect would apply late in the project.‡

You can do this too. The essence of project planning is breaking the project down into pieces small enough so that each may be sized with some degree of confidence. Once this has been done, any project management program or device, including a pocket calculator, can determine how long the project will take. Without good sizing, the project cannot be managed.

---

†Project management would require a book in itself; for further reading try Philip W. Metzger, *Managing a Programming Project* (Englewood Cliffs, NJ: Prentice-Hall, 1973), or Richard C. Gunther, *Management Methodology for Software Product Engineering* (New York: Wiley, 1978).

‡This is Brooks's law; people added late in the project serve to delay it further. From Frederick Brooks, Jr., *The Mythical Man-Month* (Reading, Mass.: Addison-Wesley, 1975), p. 25.

Shifts in Specifications

During the course of most large software projects, people will recommend alterations, usually enlargements of the scope of the project. Here are ways you might handle these recommendations:

Reject the Suggested Change

Standing firmly on the "frozen" specifications signed off by various levels of management, the project team proceeds full speed ahead. Users of the completed system complain that the design was outdated well before implementation. The project team's former co-workers admire their dedication to principles. (Let us hope the team doesn't discover, after rejecting an externally originated design change in this manner, that implementation is impossible without a design change.)

Accept the Suggested Change

The change becomes part of the system, contributing to its arrival a year late. The projects team's former co-workers agree that management has no right to punish them so harshly for being responsive to changing user needs.

192

Agree That the Change Was in the Design All Along

Here the project team has the worst of all possible worlds. The customer persuades them that they have misunderstood his needs, that their concept of the design is faulty. Additional work will be required, but the schedule will probably not be adjusted, because the customer has little sympathy for the delay. The project is assured of a late delivery. Better design reviews, followed by more careful signoffs by the customer, might have prevented this problem.

Review the Change Properly

First, put some friction in the system by designing a form, complete with signature block, to request that the change be reviewed. This will separate serious needs from trivial "why don't you paint it blue" requests. Then form a committee to review the change and include a member of the customer's staff who understands that any change will be paid for both in delayed delivery and increased cost of the product. If these two measures don't control the flow of changes, then perhaps the project needs a redesign.

Obviously no standard answer will see us through these troubled waters. Because large system development, by definition, takes some time, and because the environment the system will serve is also developing, some drifting apart will occur. Response to the drift may be necessary, but should not be undertaken lightly. The cost of discarding work in process by changing the system design must be acknowledged, as well as the cost to redo the discarded work. These costs, and the associated delays in the projects, must be weighed against the benefits of the change. Someone representing the end users' interests and the individual paying the bill for the project, working together, are usually the best people to determine if the change is required.

How does this relate to debugging? As mentioned in the chapter "Did You Use The Same Model Throughout," specification changes are often incompletely implemented, and you may have a hard time spotting the incompleteness in the code.

How do you avoid the trap? Conduct design reviews for the alteration with even more thoroughness than for the original design. Have the code read with the specific intent of finding discrepancies between old and new design. Test the affected areas of the system especially carefully.

Building Versus Buying Software

Sometimes We Must Both Build and Buy

The brochure is smart, the text reads well, the models in the pictures are gorgeous, but does this have anything to do with whether you should buy the package? Maybe, but you should ask some important questions first.

Sometimes the value of a particular package goes beyond its quality and function. If the program has some stature in the industry you may be compelled to purchase the "brand name." When the customer's contract asks for it by name, you may save yourself trouble by offering it rather than demonstrating that your home-grown package is superior.

Often the pricing for software appears outrageous. The smallest utility package may cost $100 per month per system.

195

A major system may cost five to ten times that. Your immediate reaction may be, "Heck, I can make my own for much less." Perhaps you can, but remember, early estimates for the finished product are usually very low. How often have we said, after the project is over, "If we had known total costs, we would have scrapped it in the design stage." A pessimism factor should be used to adjust for early project euphoria. One approach, devised from weapons systems work, suggests a rule of twice as long or two years longer than planned, whichever is shorter. This factor covers changes and extensions outside the original design, but required nonetheless. For more experimental kinds of work involving computing, a factor of five might be more appropriate! We can also gauge the variance of our estimate using the square root of the estimate. If the estimate is four years, a duration of between two and six years ($\sqrt{4} = 2$) should not surprise us. Use the information from Appendix C to convert person-hours to dollars.

Also, remember that the vendor is offering to *deliver* the product on a certain day, while you are considering *starting to design* your version. Does the finished product have some time value? Do you need it yesterday? When we lease software, we can begin using it immediately, while when we develop software, we cannot begin using it until the development is completed. (If the vendor offers a free test period, we can even use the package without charge for a little while!) Thus we can immediately begin matching revenue to costs. Certainly for the short term, this argument for leasing software is very strong. Finally, remember that you probably cannot instantly replace the people you assign to developing your version of the product. You must decide if writing software you could purchase is the best use of your staff.

Alternatively, ego may discourage you from examining inexpensive products: "Heck, if it costs so little, it cannot be a quality product like we can make ourselves." Separate out cost: determine if the product would be used if available. If not, you needn't worry about price.

How do you know you aren't buying a lemon? Ask the person who owns one. Getting people to talk about a software package they are using is like pushing on an open door. Ten minutes of discussion with a current user is worth hours of reading the program documentation. The user can put the package's features and shortcomings into perspective. The telephone is your best friend here. User groups are often good places to ask about software packages; usually you can find someone familiar with even the most obscure package. Or, you can ask the vendor for references. A friend of mine did and then called the first reference, who assured him that no one in his right mind would purchase the package! Don't assume the vendor's references are biased; even if they like the package, they can give you valuable insights. Don't forget to find out if anyone is using the product in a configuration or environment similar to yours.

Review the conditions of the license agreement with your legal people. Are you making unexpected commitments? If you modify the software, who owns the modification? What is said about using the package on multiple systems?

Another sort of reference you will need is a financial reference. You need to know whether the vendor will fold within the month.

Ask about support. How often will new versions be distributed? How will the maintenance be distributed? What happens if you suffer a program problem? Are program operation or user classes available? What is the vendor's maintenance position if you modify the package, or the operating system it runs on? As a relative of the support issue, you should determine how the decision to buy a product locks you in. Can you migrate from the product if your needs or environment change, or are you stuck with it? What are your back-off possibilities?

Get answers to all these questions, and you will find that making the build-versus-buy decision won't be too difficult.

Teamwork

Managers often speak glowingly of their systems programming "team." Is this concept realistic? In a presentation† at SHARE, one participant touched on this issue.

Part of the planning process was influenced by the fact that systems programmers always underestimate. I can say that—I'm a systems programmer myself. We are the most optimistic people in data processing as long as things are going well. We have all worked so successfully in crisis so often that it tends to dictate our thinking about how long it will take to complete a task, and we tend to forget that when there's no crisis we go home at 5:00, we don't work weekends, and we stop occasionally for a cup of coffee.

We definitely did have problems within the systems programming group. This is a delicate issue, I know, but it had impact on our conversion effort. Conversions of this size can and did point where the group was not functioning smoothly as a human organization. Prior to MVS conversion, we'd had signals—projects would slip anywhere from a week to a month, but because there was so little interdependence, the slippage had little effect. With MVS, we now have a whole network of interdependence—if one project slips by a month, we have potential to delay the entire conversion effort by six months or more. At least we know enough now to watch for breakdowns in communications, and we will be spending almost 30% of our time in the future monitoring our group health. . . .

†Patience Rochester, "MVS User Experiences in Conversion," (SHARE 45, New York, August 1975). ©1975 by SHARE, Inc., reprinted by permission.

I'll end with this last point which we feel to be the most important. We're learning to plan for organizational stress in a conversion of this type. We, and by we, I mean data processing professionals in general, tend to minimize the non-quantifiable aspects of our work. But just as more people must become involved when the computing world changes radically, it behooves us to remember that they are *people*, not machines which we also work. MVS conversion certainly needn't tear an installation apart, but there will be trauma. The only way to minimize it is to acknowledge it and plan for it.

My own company-sponsored training reflects the growing attention teamwork is receiving. During my first six years with the company, I attended eight classes, only one of which had to do with working with others. Since it was only an eight-hour class, by comparing classroom hours, only about 3 percent of my company-sponsored training was in interpersonal relations. The rest was strictly technical. My more recent experience reflects the shift in emphasis: in nine years with the company, four of thirteen classes relate to teamwork issues, totaling 24 percent of my company-sponsored class time.

Often the focus of success and failure of projects is on the managers. How good was the leadership on the effort? What, beyond inspiring words and regular paychecks, nurtures a team feeling among the staff?

I have long tenure with my company; I understand the average stay at the job in this industry is about two years. Can a group of individuals who have worked together usually for less than two years, with little training in professional cooperation, be called a team?

Follow Patience's advice and devote time to monitoring group health, making sure that the "team" is working together. Use the techniques from the chapter on "Top Down Implementation" to assure that as much time as possible is available for resolving communication problems.

Using a New Systems Programmer

When a new systems programmer joins the organization, we must balance our desire to put the individual to work with the risk of giving him too difficult an assignment. Whether the new person is a trainee or an experienced veteran, we usually don't know his exact level of skill.

Small Steps

The first task assigned to the new systems programmer should be relatively small. Just as in programming courses, the educational and emotional benefits of a large, half-finished project are nil. Satisfaction, learning, and the feeling of belonging come from completed tasks, so keep things small at first.

Reviews

Design walkthroughs and code inspections, important for any project, provide deep insight into the work habits of the new individual. For the new staffer, we conduct more reviews than his normally small first project would demand. Reading one program is worth dozens of resumes. See the chapter on "Structured Walkthroughs."

Safety

No manager wants to be known for hiring a systems programmer whose first month's work caused ten system failures. That systems programmer won't enjoy the reputation, either, so keep the first project relatively safe. Avoid tasks that require disabling memory protection or machine interrupts, or updating important data files. Read-only utilities are nearly ideal assignments for safety and we always need more of them, so the work assignment can be made "real." See the chapter on "Extract Routines" for some further ideas.

Integrating a new systems programmer into the organization can be traumatic, both for the individual and the organization, but we can take steps to reduce the trauma in duration and magnitude, and speed the individual's move from "new kid" to co-worker status.

The Annual Report

A professional career, like any other human activity, requires management and direction for best results. A written annual report, submitted to your management, affords a valuable assessment of your activities.

My employer's personnel evaluation procedures include the annual report, but for years I didn't use it to best advantage: when asked about my activities, I wrote one sentence, "I support HASP."

Once I reflected on the nature of our organization, I realized two important facts: first-level supervisors change jobs faster than workers and good supervisors usually don't have time for extensive detective or historical work about all the things their people do for the common good.

Writing a good annual report takes all year! As major activities begin and end, log them. When someone writes you a memo telling you what a good job you did, save it with your log. If someone comes by and *tells* you what a good job you did, encourage them to write it down and send a copy to your supervisor. (A corollary to this encourages you to write bouquet memos yourself for people who have done you a good turn. Since so much of the memo traffic can be negative, the bouquet memos stand out.)

The log and the bouquets are the raw material of your annual report. I aim for a one- to two-page report, with a "major accomplishments" section, listing the two or three activities everyone would agree were along the main line of the organization's efforts. I list "lessor activities" and include the things

I did that didn't make the majors list. After each item on both lists, I discuss briefly just what I did. I reference the bouquet memos, and attach copies after my summary.

Once the report is written, two reviews must be held. First, *you* must review it to determine if the activities on the list were what you wanted to spend this year of your life doing. Armed with this knowledge, you are ready to review the report with your manager.

Several things can come out of this meeting. (I say meeting, because the review is serious business and should be scheduled and kept private and interrupt-free to the extent the environment allows.) Your manager may recall activities that you had forgotten to mention. A forgotten activity in the majors list may indicate you and your manager disagree about your work assignment: this should be resolved. Finally, if you found that your career isn't going where you want, you should bring this up. (Be cautioned that you are taking a risk: if the kind of work you wish to do isn't available, you will either have to live with what you have or change jobs.)

A business that doesn't take inventory periodically will go bankrupt. A career requires similar assessment. The annual report requires only a few hours a year, and provides you with invaluable knowledge about where your professional life is headed. Try it out.

Firefighting Without Burning Out

Perhaps the worst side of systems programming is the 3:00 A.M. telephone call from the computer operator, reporting that the system cannot be restarted. Although the prevention and diagnosis themes of this book should help you move away from crisis management, there are also ways to ease the tension and troubles associated with a crisis.

Bring Your Toolbag

Systems programmers are the only repairmen I know of who routinely travel to work without tools. Although we may not need a physical "tool-kit," we shouldn't enter the machine room hoping to resolve a system failure unarmed. What are the tools?

- Hand Calculator (See "Automating the Arithmetic")
- System Resource Monitor (See "Instrumentation")
- Interactive Debugger (See "Special Debugging Tools")
- Dump Formatter (See "Special Debugging Tools")
- Program Listings. Obviously, program listings should be available when trying to resolve a machine problem. If you are considering on-line storage of computer listings, make some provision for listing availability when the machine is down, or you will have painted yourself into a corner. Microfiche achieves the same space economies, without relying on a working computer for retrieval. While I was temporarily located a mile from the computer, over highways used heavily during rush hours, I developed the habit of carrying program listings in my car, so that I would have what listings I needed with me when I arrived.
- Alternate Systems. Often, if the production operating system will not start up properly, a simple and helpful test is to start an alternate system that doesn't rely on data on the production system disks. This test will quickly help separate hardware and software problems; if the alternate system starts properly, the production system is sick, while if the alternate won't start either, the computing equipment could well be broken. With spooling systems, a secondary spooling disk, different from the production disks, allows us to use the system to diagnose and repair damage on the main spool disks.
- Data File Display Programs. Often, our problem is caused by bad data on a system data file, for example, the spooling disks. An alternate program can be a powerful tool for isolating the damage. Such programs can be as simple as a disk dump program, or complicated and powerful enough to trace and format the control block chains involved and automatically report illogical sequences.

Know Your Objectives

Working with a limping system in the middle of the night can be doubly difficult if you haven't a clear picture of what you hope to achieve. When working with problems associated with the spooling system, I follow two major guidelines, as laid out by managment:

1. *Restore the Service as Quickly as Possible.* Since our customers depend on our service, and we depend on customer revenue, this is basic.
2. *Protect Spooled Data from Loss.* Protecting spooled data is slightly less important than quick service restoration. We would rather delete a damaged job on the system and refund the run than delay another few minutes attempting reconstruction. On the other hand, we will spend a few minutes exploring correction techniques before choosing to cold-start and delete all the jobs on the queue.

Knowing the guidelines is terribly important, because they affect your actions. Your management should be polled for this information; my preceding guidelines may be inappropriate or irrelevant to your operation.

Into Action

You enter the machine room, follow your usual debugging techniques, and eventually discover what is wrong. You may have found a hardware problem, or perhaps a subtle software failure. You may make a patch to system software to return the system to service. When writing such a patch, make it as small and safe as possible. Don't overestimate your ability to reprogram in a crisis, or you will pay the consequences.

Afterwards

Reading a book my stepson has on Little League pitching, I found some marvelous advice: if you pitch a win, enjoy it to the hilt; wallow in it! If, on the other hand, you pitch a loss, don't brood on it. Put the past behind you.

If you quickly and successfully returned the system to service, review your clever plans, and good moves. Enjoy! If, however, things went poorly, and you spent two hours finding a problem you realized later should have taken you only ten minutes, remember that you did the best you could with the information available and the level of sleep you had at the time. (Why do these things so often occur in the middle of the night?)

Finally, formulate a plan to prevent the failure from recurring. Don't waste a system failure; learn what is necessary to eliminate, or at least speed diagnosis of the problem. Some of the best motivation for system instrumentation appears the morning after an all-night session with a system problem.

Demonstrations

Few activities can be more stressful than demonstrating a system. As I write this, I recall a recent experience: meeting a friend in the hall, I said, "Come and see my new terminal." I pressed start and the device had an immediate machine error! There are ways you can minimize your risk at demonstrations and avoid the embarrassment I suffered.

Material Advantage

Just as in chess, where this term originates, demonstrations go easier if you can overwhelm them with equipment. If you need one terminal, bring two. If you think you will need a little paper or some tape, bring lots along. If the terminal uses ribbons or type elements, bring along a handful of spares. If your terminal is so large that duplicates aren't feasible, or you need many functional terminals, arrange to have the vendor's engineer on site to correct hiccups.

Communications

As a general rule, prepare and rehearse whatever you plan to do well ahead of time. If data communications are involved, make doubly sure that the lines you need are available and functional. In particular, remember that hotel switchboards are often incapable of carrying data traffic, even though they work perfectly for voice communications.

Don't Do Anything Real

Keep the plan for your demonstration as modest as the requirements allow. Your risk increases as you move from using standard production systems to new developmental and experimental systems. Try to plan for a backup demonstration, even more modest than your original idea, to further reduce risk.

I was involved in registration for a large (3000 attendee) computer conference, and successfully steered us away from on-line interactive registration. We used prepunched cards for pre-registered attendees, and fully manual registration methods. Registration was a huge success.

Load the Dice

In an interactive environment, demonstrations are often improved if the normally democratic technique of distributing computer resources is abridged. Favor the demonstration sessions and jobs with higher priority. Limit the overall system load. If the demonstration is important to management, they will support and encourage these adjustments. Remember, you want to show your system off at its best.

These measures will not eliminate the risk associated with demonstrations, but they will control those things you can control. Good luck!

Follow-up

1. Arrange to attend a "User Group Meeting." Write a "Conference Trip Report" discussing the benefits you realized, and deliver it to your boss.

2. Write an "Annual Report" without waiting for a year's collection of data. (You may have to rely on your memory.) Review the report with your boss to see if you agree about the last year's events.

3. How do you handle emergencies? Do you use any or all of the techniques mentioned in "Firefighting Without Burning Out?"

4. Review the questions in "Building Versus Buying Software" and rate each on a scale from 1 (most important) to 5 (least important) for your installation. Then evaluate a software package using these ground rules.

Afterword

Throughout the book I have stressed techniques for reducing debugging problems and ways of preventing the errors that force us to debug. Improved productivity will result from successful use of these methods. Productivity is important to data processing for two reasons: first, because productivity in general provides the only true improvement in standard of living, and second, because data processing productivity must improve if the industry can meet the demands of the future.

Summary of Data Processing Industry Trends[†] (Normalized to 1955)				
Indicator	1955	1965	1975	1985
Industry Growth	1	20	80	320
Performance/cost	1	10^2	10^4	10^6
Programmer productivity	1	2.0	2.7	3.6
System reliability	1	5	24	120

As this table clearly shows, programmer productivity, the rate at which logic structures are manufactured, has not improved

[†]Taken from T. A. Dolotta, et al., *Data Processing in 1980–1985* (New York: Wiley, 1976), p. 175, Table B.4. ©1976 by SHARE, Inc., reprinted by permission.

as rapidly as other important aspects of the industry. The time has come for programming to catch up. The methods described in this book will allow you to work more rapidly, both because you will debug more quickly, and because you will adopt programming techniques that produce fewer bugs.

APPENDIX A

Enqueue Lockout Prevention

Havender† offers four approaches to designing out lockout problems:

APPROACH 1. In designing a program, request a resource for a task while another resource has been allocated to it only if it can be demonstrated that no other group of interlocking tasks will exist concurrently that (1) have been allocated the requested resource and (2) will later require the resources allocated to the original task. Simply stated, ensure that resources are requested for all tasks in the same order.

If, as is often the case, the first approach is not applicable, there are three alternatives:

APPROACH 2. Request resources collectively. Do not proceed with the task until all required resources have been obtained.

APPROACH 3. If holding a formerly obtained resource may prevent acquisition of an additional resource, release the original resource before obtaining the additional resource. If the original resource is still required, re-request it collectively with the additional resource.

APPROACH 4. When a request for a resource is denied and when Approach 1 is not applicable, be prepared to take an alternative course of action. Do not wait for the needed resource while retaining other resources.

---

†J. W. Havender, "Avoiding Deadlock in Multitasking Systems," IBM *Systems Journal* 7, no. 2 (1968), p. 78. Reprinted by permission from the IBM Systems Journal. ©1968 by International Business Machines Corporation.

To which, I would add:

> APPROACH 5. To prevent performance and lockout problems in tasks that provide resources or support real-time or on-line applications, queue resource requests and have a subtask process the queue.

To translate what we did into Havender's terms, eliminating the TSO request to lock the region in memory is approach 4. Without the region lock-in, SMF proceeded normally, and HASP was never stuck behind a locked-out TSO session.

Using a subtask to handle SMF requests in HASP is approach 5, of course. (Approach 5 is an expansion of approach 4, since the subtasking allows main-line processing to continue.

APPENDIX B

Assembler Language Danger Areas

1. Branches in pairs
2. Backwards branches
3. Routines longer than a listing page
4. Operands on xxC/xxI instructions (MVC/MVI)
5. Conflicting instruction and data field widths
6. Mask operand on 370 mask instructions
7. Comments on the END statement
8. Length and register fields on xxC instructions (MVC)
9. LA versus L instruction
10. Literal pool positioning
11. TEMP variables
12. Positive branches heavily used
13. Memory protection suspensions
14. Access controls for new SVCs
15. Reentrancy rules followed
16. Dynamic instruction modification avoided
17. Special instruction sets avoided
18. Memory management planning
19. Comments sufficient for coding
20. Language processor diagnostics
21. Program version reporting
22. Use of the location counter (*)
23. Mapping macros instead of absolute offsets

24. Device dependent code avoids local tables
25. Character counts correct or eliminated
26. Assembly parameters avoided for program logic
27. Use of the correct base register

This checklist was extracted from the "Coding Practices" and "Keeping it Symbolic" sections and the "Trampled Data" chapter of the book. The reader will wish to read those sections and that chapter before using this list.

APPENDIX C

Economics of Systems Programmers

Our hypothetical systems programmer earns about $24,000† and costs the company at least as much in indirect costs: the benefits package, vacation and sick leave, and office space come to mind. That divides out to $182 a week or $23 an hour.

Systems programming requires working with changing technology, and the cost of continuing education is not included in these figures.

---

†From Source EDP, "1980 Computer Salary Survey." Source EDP, 100 South Wacker Drive, Chicago, IL 60606.

GLOSSARY

Bebugging: Installing preplanned bugs in a program or system prior to testing to permit assessment of test effectiveness.

Breakpoints: Temporary traps installed in a program using a debugger. When the trap is reached, control is passed to the debugger.

Deadly Embrace: Another name for a resource lockout or enqueue lockout, frequently used in the computer science literature.

Debugger: A program, usually interactive, used to test programs. Usually supports storage and register display and alteration, and the temporary installation of traps, often called breakpoints, which invoke the debugger when activated. Some debuggers use compiler or assembler produced symbol tables, permitting debugging by variable names, and some will permit trapping on register or storage alteration, or tracing program execution.

Dump: A print of the contents of main or auxiliary memory.

Exit: A subroutine that tailors a package to specific needs without requiring other program modification.

Eyecatcher: A data field within program code and data area intended for easy recognition when examining storage.

Hard-Wiring: Making a program dependent specific configuration characteristics.

Inspection: A review of program coding conducted with the help of professionals not involved in the coding task.

Instrumentation: Coding within a program that captures performance information about the program as it operates.

Integrity: The ability of an operating system to protect itself from unauthorized requests for privileged services.

JES2: Job Entry Subsystem 2, a spooling system for MVS. JES2 controls all local unit record devices and remote batch teleprocessing sessions on the system.

MVS: Multiple Virtual Storages, the large-scale operating system for the IBM System/370. MVS uses virtual memory to provide batch and time-sharing services to many users concurrently.

Scripts: Lists of terminal system commands, executed automatically, usually for system performance measurement.

Security: The ability of an operating system to prevent unauthorized use of protected data. An aspect of integrity.

SMF: System Management Facility, the accounting system for OS/VS. Each system component prepares accounting information and passes it to SMF for writing to disk storage.

Super-Zap: On OS/360 and OS/VS systems, the utility used for, and thus the practice of making, absolute changes to programs or data files.

System Build: A time-honored system development technique: after the system is designed and the modules are coded and tested in isolation, the complete system is constructed by combination.

Trap: Code within a program that detects unusual conditions and takes special actions. Normally written and installed when pursuing a program error.

Walkthrough: A review of program design, conducted partly by professionals not involved in the design process, intended to disclose design errors prior to programming.

Index

A

Abending, 98
Absolute patches, 20
Annual report, 202
Assembler language, 156
Assembly parameters, 156
Attitudes about errors, 188
Automatic correction, 104

B

Batch jobs, 103
Bebugging, 189, 219
Bounties, for bugs, 177
Branch ratio, 125
Branch, test every, 169
Breakpoints, 13, 219
Build vs. buy, 195
Buying software, 195

C

Calculations, 29
Career assessment, 202
Cases, test, 169
Changes, 19, 34, 111, 141, 165
Changes:
    recent, 10
    specification, 192
Checking, validity, 7
Code inspection, 70

Code reading, 33, 215
Comments, 136
Communications, 208
Console logs, 50
Control blocks, 5, 149
Cost of testing, 26
Counting characters, 154
Current location counter, 147

D

Data extract routines, 53
Data file testing, 172
Dataset security, 108
Dead fish, 125
Deadly embrace, 30, 219
Debugger, dynamic, 13, 219
Decision tables, 92, 169
Demonstrations, 208
Device dependency, 151
Diagnostics, 139
Diagnostics program, 39
Difficult documentation, 181
Documentation:
    system, 61, 173
    user, 88
Doing too much, 190
Dump program, 113
Dump reading, 11
Dumps, 9, 49, 219

E
Efficiency, 73, 83
END statement, 122
Enqueue lockouts, 30, 213
Error handling, 98
Error lists, 27
Error messages, 95
Error reporting, 28, 63
Errors, ideas about, 188
Exit, 13, 111, 219
Extract routines, 53
Eyecatcher, 72, 142, 219

F
Failure recovery, 85
Fast clocks, 167
Fast counters, 167
Field sizes, 121
Flowcharts, 90
Free time, for testing, 176
Frequency distributions, 173

H
Hardware, 54, 56
Hardware problems, 36
Hard-wiring, 145, 219
Help, 27, 182
High level languages, 79
Home terminals, 58
Humane input, 101

I
Independent testing, 175
Initiators, 113
Inspection, code, 70, 220
Instruction modification, 131
Instructions, special, 133
Instrumentation, 16, 220
Integrity, 127, 186, 220
Interfaces, 106
Invalid address, 11

J
JES2, 220
Jobs, 113

K
Keep it simple, 209

L
Large projects, 191, 198
Length operand, 123
Literal pool, 123–124
Literals, 120–121
Location counter, 147
Lockouts, enqueue, 30, 213
Logic manuals, 63
Logs, fix and failure, 51
Loops, 42, 43

M
Making it beautiful, 190
Manuals, 61
Mapping macros, 149
Mask instructions, 121–122
Memory management, 134
Memory protection, 63, 126
Messages:
  console, 50
  error, 95
  generation, 154
  response, 99
Methodic testing, 175
Modularity, 111
MVS, 220

N
Negative branches, 125

O
Operator commands, 87
Operator procedures, 47
Original function testing, 165
Overengineering, 190
Overlaid data, 5

P
Patches, 20
Path testing, 169
Pattern recognition, 9, 40
Performance, 16, 22, 73, 75, 83
Peripherals, 54
Planning the test, 161
Portability, 81
Positive branches, 125
Problem reporting, 52

Processor recovery, 85
Productivity, 211
Program evaluation, 195
Program instrumentation, 16
Program planning, 71
Program portability, 81
Programmimg language, 79, 81,
   120, 139
Programming, reentrant, 129
Project planning, 191

Q
Quick error tests, 125
Quirks of assembler, 120

R
Range checking, 172
Reading code, 33, 136, 215
Reading dumps, 11
Recent changes, 10
Redesign, 17
Redundancy, data file, 173
Reentrancy, 129
Register contents, 123
Register saving, 41
Regression, 165
Resources, 16, 30, 77, 171, 213
Responsive messages, 99
Restrictive environments, 168
Retesting, 166

S
Save areas, 41
Scripts, 176, 220
Security, dataset, 108, 220
Short routines, 119
Simulation, 113
SMF, 30, 220
Software maintenance, 27
Sorts, 173
Spare parts, 208
Special instructions, 133
Specification, changes, 192
Statistical techniques, 173–174
Storage, 134
Stress testing, 171

Structured programming, 119
Structured walkthrough, 69, 181
Sunset support, 109
Super-zap, 20, 220
Support personnel, 28
Support, vendor, 27
System build, 107, 220
System documentation, 181
System testing, 176

T
Teamwork, 198
TEMP variables, 125
Terminals, 56, 58
Termination, 109
Test planning, 161
Test simulators, 176
Timing, 35
Tools, 13, 53, 54, 56, 71,
   126, 176
Top down implementation, 106
Tracing program, 14
Tracking, 51
Traps, 7, 220
Trip report, 184
Tuning, 209

U
Unconditional branches, 119
Updates, manual, 61–62
User documentation, 88
User errors, 101, 104
Users meetings, 182, 184
Using manuals, 63

V
Validity checking, 7
Vendor support, 27
Version information, 141

W
Walkthrough, 69, 220

Z
Zaps, 20